Amazon MQ Developer Guide

A catalogue record for this book is available from the Hong Kong Public Libraries.

Published in Hong Kong by Samurai Media Limited.

Email: info@samuraimedia.org

ISBN 9789888408160

Contents

What Is Amazon MQ?

Amazon MQ is a managed message broker service for Apache ActiveMQ that makes it easy to migrate to a message broker in the cloud. A *message broker* allows software applications and components to communicate using various programming languages, operating systems, and formal messaging protocols.

Amazon MQ works with your existing applications and services without the need to manage, operate, or maintain your own messaging system.

- What Are the Main Benefits of Amazon MQ?
- How is Amazon MQ Different from Amazon SQS or Amazon SNS?
- How Can I Get Started with Amazon MQ?
- We Want to Hear from You

What Are the Main Benefits of Amazon MQ?

- **Security** – You control who can create and modify brokers and who can send messages to and receive messages from an ActiveMQ broker. Amazon MQ encrypts messages at rest and in transit using encryption keys that it manages and stores securely.

- **Durability** – To ensure the safety of your messages, Amazon MQ stores them on redundant shared storage.

- **Availability** – You can create a single-instance broker (comprised of one broker in one Availability Zone), or an active/standby broker for high availability (comprised of two brokers in two different Availability Zones). For either broker type, Amazon MQ automatically provisions infrastructure for high availability.

- **Enterprise readiness** – Amazon MQ supports industry-standard APIs and protocols so you can migrate from your existing message broker without rewriting application code.

- **Operation offloading** – You can configure many aspects of your ActiveMQ broker, such as predefined destinations, destination policies, authorization policies, and plugins. Amazon MQ controls some of these configuration elements, such as network transports and storage, simplifying the maintenance and administration of your messaging system in the cloud.

How Is Amazon MQ Different from Amazon SQS or Amazon SNS?

Amazon MQ is a managed message broker service that provides compatibility with many popular message brokers. We recommend Amazon MQ for migrating applications from existing message brokers that rely on compatibility with APIs such as JMS or protocols such as AMQP, MQTT, OpenWire, and STOMP.

Amazon SQS and Amazon SNS are queue and topic services that are highly scalable, simple to use, and don't require you to set up message brokers. We recommend these services for new applications that can benefit from nearly unlimited scalability and simple APIs.

How Can I Get Started with Amazon MQ?

- To create your first broker with Amazon MQ, see Getting Started with Amazon MQ.

- To discover the functionality and architecture of Amazon MQ, see How Amazon MQ Works.

- To find out the guidelines and caveats that will help you make the most of Amazon MQ, see Best Practices for Amazon MQ.

- To learn about Amazon MQ REST APIs, see the *Amazon MQ REST API Reference.*

- To learn about Amazon MQ AWS CLI commands, see Amazon MQ in the *AWS CLI Command Reference.*

We Want to Hear from You

We welcome your feedback. To contact us, visit the Amazon MQ Discussion Forum.

Frequently Viewed Amazon MQ Topics

Latest update: May 4, 2018

Amazon MQ Developer Guide	Amazon MQ REST API Reference
[See the AWS documentation website for more details]	[See the AWS documentation website for more details]

Setting Up Amazon MQ

Before you can use Amazon MQ, you must complete the following steps.

- Create an AWS Account and an IAM Administrator User
- Create an IAM User and Get Your AWS Credentials
- Get Ready to Use the Example Code
- Next Steps

Step 1: Create an AWS Account and an IAM Administrator User

To access any AWS service, you must first create an AWS account. This is an Amazon account that can use AWS products. You can use your AWS account to view your activity and usage reports and to manage authentication and access.

1. Navigate to the AWS home page, and then choose **Create an AWS Account**.

2. Follow the instructions.

   Part of the sign-up procedure involves receiving a phone call and entering a PIN using the phone keypad.

3. When you finish creating your AWS account, follow the instructions in the *IAM User Guide* to create your first IAM administrator user and group.

Step 2: Create an IAM User and Get Your AWS Credentials

To avoid using your IAM administrator user for Amazon MQ operations, it is a best practice to create an IAM user for each person who needs administrative access to Amazon MQ.

To work with Amazon MQ, you need the `AmazonMQFullAccess` policy and AWS credentials that are associated with your IAM user. These credentials are comprised of an access key ID and a secret access key. For more information, see What Is IAM? in the *IAM User Guide* and AWS Security Credentials in the *AWS General Reference*.

1. Sign in to the AWS Identity and Access Management console.

2. Choose **Users**, **Add user**.

3. Type a **User name**, such as `AmazonMQAdmin`.

4. Select **Programmatic access** and **AWS Management Console access**.

5. Set a **Console password** and then choose **Next: Permissions**.

6. On the **Set permissions for *AmazonMQAdmin*** page, choose **Attach existing policies directly**.

7. Type `AmazonMQ` into the filter, choose **AmazonMQFullAccess**, and then choose **Next: Review**.

8. On the **Review** page, choose **Create user**.

   The IAM user is created and the **Access key ID** is displayed, for example:

   AKIAIOSFODNN7EXAMPLE

9. To display your **Secret access key**, choose **Show**, for example:

   wJalrXUtnFEMI/K7MDENG/bPxRfiCYEXAMPLEKEY Important
   You can view or download your secret access key *only* when you create your credentials (however, you can create new credentials at any time).

10. To download your credentials, choose **Download .csv**. Keep this file in a secure location.

Step 3: Get Ready to Use the Example Code

The following tutorials show how you can work with Amazon MQ and ActiveMQ using the AWS Management Console and Java. To use the example code, you must install the Java Standard Edition Development Kit and make some changes to the code.

You can also create and manage brokers programmatically using Amazon MQ REST API and AWS SDKs.

Next Steps

Now that you're prepared to work with Amazon MQ, get started by creating a broker and then connecting a Java application to your broker.

Getting Started with Amazon MQ

This section will help you become more familiar with Amazon MQ by showing you how to create a broker and how to connect your application to it.

- Prerequisites
- Create an ActiveMQ Broker
- Connect a Java Application to Your Broker
- Delete Your Broker
- Next Steps

Prerequisites

Before you begin, complete the steps in Setting Up Amazon MQ.

Step 1: Create an ActiveMQ Broker

A *broker* is a message broker environment running on Amazon MQ. It is the basic building block of Amazon MQ. The combined description of the broker instance *class* (`m4`, `t2`) and *size* (`large`, `micro`) is a *broker instance type* (for example, `mq.m4.large`). For more information, see Broker.

The first and most common Amazon MQ task is creating a broker. The following example shows how you can use the AWS Management Console to create a basic broker.

1. Sign in to the Amazon MQ console.

2. Do one of the following:

   - If this is your first time using Amazon MQ, in the **Create a broker** section, type `MyBroker` for **Broker name** and then choose **Next step**.

   - If you have created a broker before, on the **Create a broker** page, in the **Broker details** section, type `MyBroker` for **Broker name**.

3. Choose a **Broker instance type** (for example, **mq.m4.large**). For more information, see Instance Types.

4. For **Deployment mode**, ensure that **Single-instance broker** is selected. **Note** Currently, Amazon MQ supports only the `ActiveMQ` broker engine, version `5.15.0`.

5. In the **ActiveMQ Web Console access** section, type a **Username** and **Password**.

6. Choose **Create broker**.

   While Amazon MQ creates your broker, it displays the **Creation in progress** status.

   Creating the broker takes about 15 minutes.

   When your broker is created successfully, Amazon MQ displays the **Running** status.

Name	Status	Deployment mode	Instance type
MyBroker	Running	Single-instance broker	mq.m4.large

7. Choose *MyBroker*.

   On the *MyBroker* page, in the **Connect** section, note your broker's **ActiveMQ Web Console** URL, for example:

```
1 https://b-1234a5b6-78cd-901e-2fgh-3i45j6k17819-1.mq.us-east-2.amazonaws.com:8162
```

Also, note your broker's wire-level protocol **Endpoints**. The following is an example of an OpenWire endpoint:

```
1 ssl://b-1234a5b6-78cd-901e-2fgh-3i45j6k17819-1.mq.us-east-2.amazonaws.com:61617
```

Step 2: Connect a Java Application to Your Broker

After you create an Amazon MQ broker, you can connect your application to it. The following examples show how you can use the Java Message Service (JMS) to create a connection to the broker, create a queue, and send a message. For a complete, working Java example, see Working Examples of Using Java Message Service (JMS) with ActiveMQ.

You can connect to ActiveMQ brokers using various ActiveMQ clients. We recommend using the ActiveMQ Client.

Important
To ensure that your broker is accessible within your VPC, you must enable the `enableDnsHostnames` and `enableDnsSupport` VPC attributes. For more information, see DNS Support in your VPC in the *Amazon VPC User Guide*.

Prerequisites

Add the `activemq-client.jar` and `activemq-pool.jar` packages to your Java class path. The following example shows these dependencies in a Maven project `pom.xml` file.

```
1  <dependencies>
2      <dependency>
3          <groupId>org.apache.activemq</groupId>
4          <artifactId>activemq-client</artifactId>
5          <version>5.15.0</version>
6      </dependency>
7      <dependency>
8          <groupId>org.apache.activemq</groupId>
9          <artifactId>activemq-pool</artifactId>
10         <version>5.15.0</version>
11     </dependency>
12 </dependencies>
```

For more information about `activemq-client.jar`, see Initial Configuration in the Apache ActiveMQ documentation.

Create a Message Producer and Send a Message

1. Create a JMS pooled connection factory for the message producer using your broker's endpoint and then call the `createConnection` method against the factory. **Note**
   For an active/standby broker for high availability, Amazon MQ provides two ActiveMQ Web Console URLs, but only one URL is active at a time. Likewise, Amazon MQ provides two endpoints for each wire-level protocol, but only one endpoint is active in each pair at a time. The -1 and -2 suffixes denote a redundant pair. For more information, see Amazon MQ Broker Architecture).
   For wire-level protocol endpoints, you can allow your application to connect to either endpoint by using the Failover Transport.

```
1  // Create a connection factory.
2  final ActiveMQConnectionFactory connectionFactory = new ActiveMQConnectionFactory(
       wireLevelEndpoint);
3
4  // Pass the username and password.
5  connectionFactory.setUserName(activeMqUsername);
6  connectionFactory.setPassword(activeMqPassword);
7
8  // Create a pooled connection factory.
9  final PooledConnectionFactory pooledConnectionFactory = new PooledConnectionFactory();
10 pooledConnectionFactory.setConnectionFactory(connectionFactory);
11 pooledConnectionFactory.setMaxConnections(10);
12
13 // Establish a connection for the producer.
14 final Connection producerConnection = pooledConnectionFactory.createConnection();
15 producerConnection.start();
```

Note

Message producers should always use the `PooledConnectionFactory` class. For more information, see Always Use Connection Pooling.

1. Create a session, a queue named `MyQueue`, and a message producer.

```
1  // Create a session.
2  final Session producerSession = producerConnection.createSession(false, Session.
       AUTO_ACKNOWLEDGE);
3
4  // Create a queue named "MyQueue".
5  final Destination producerDestination = producerSession.createQueue("MyQueue");
6
7  // Create a producer from the session to the queue.
8  final MessageProducer producer = producerSession.createProducer(producerDestination);
9  producer.setDeliveryMode(DeliveryMode.NON_PERSISTENT);
```

2. Create the message string `"Hello from Amazon MQ!"` and then send the message.

```
1  // Create a message.
2  final String text = "Hello from Amazon MQ!";
3  TextMessage producerMessage = producerSession.createTextMessage(text);
4
5  // Send the message.
6  producer.send(producerMessage);
7  System.out.println("Message sent.");
```

3. Clean up the producer.

```
1  producer.close();
2  producerSession.close();
3  producerConnection.close();
```

Create a Message Consumer and Receive the Message

1. Create a JMS connection factory for the message producer using your broker's endpoint and then call the `createConnection` method against the factory.

14

```
1 // Create a connection factory.
2 final ActiveMQConnectionFactory connectionFactory = new ActiveMQConnectionFactory(
    wireLevelEndpoint);
3
4 // Pass the username and password.
5 connectionFactory.setUserName(activeMqUsername);
6 connectionFactory.setPassword(activeMqPassword);
7
8 // Establish a connection for the consumer.
9 final Connection consumerConnection = connectionFactory.createConnection();
10 consumerConnection.start();
```

Note

Message consumers should *never* use the `PooledConnectionFactory` class. For more information, see Always Use Connection Pooling.

1. Create a session, a queue named `MyQueue`, and a message consumer.

```
1 // Create a session.
2 final Session consumerSession = consumerConnection.createSession(false, Session.
    AUTO_ACKNOWLEDGE);
3
4 // Create a queue named "MyQueue".
5 final Destination consumerDestination = consumerSession.createQueue("MyQueue");
6
7 // Create a message consumer from the session to the queue.
8 final MessageConsumer consumer = consumerSession.createConsumer(consumerDestination);
```

2. Begin to wait for messages and receive the message when it arrives.

```
1 // Begin to wait for messages.
2 final Message consumerMessage = consumer.receive(1000);
3
4 // Receive the message when it arrives.
5 final TextMessage consumerTextMessage = (TextMessage) consumerMessage;
6 System.out.println("Message received: " + consumerTextMessage.getText());
```

Note

Unlike AWS messaging services (such as Amazon SQS), the consumer is constantly connected to the broker.

1. Close the consumer, session, and connection.

```
1 consumer.close();
2 consumerSession.close();
3 consumerConnection.close();
4 pooledConnectionFactory.stop();
```

Step 3: Delete Your Broker

If you don't use an Amazon MQ broker (and don't foresee using it in the near future), it is a best practice to delete it from Amazon MQ to reduce your AWS costs.

The following example shows how you can delete a broker using the AWS Management Console.

1. Sign in to the Amazon MQ console.

2. From the broker list, select your broker (for example, **MyBroker**) and then choose **Delete**.

3. In the **Delete *MyBroker*?** dialog box, type `delete` and then choose **Delete**.

   Deleting a broker takes about 5 minutes.

Next Steps

Now that you have created a broker, connected an application to it, and sent and received a message, you might want to try the following:

- Tutorial: Creating and Configuring an Amazon MQ Broker (Advanced Settings)
- Tutorial: Creating and Applying Amazon MQ Broker Configurations
- Tutorial: Editing Amazon MQ Broker Configurations and Managing Configuration Revisions
- Tutorial: Listing Amazon MQ Brokers and Viewing Broker Details
- Tutorial: Creating and Managing Amazon MQ Broker Users
- Tutorial: Rebooting an Amazon MQ Broker
- Tutorial: Accessing CloudWatch Metrics for Amazon MQ

You can also begin to dive deep into Amazon MQ best practices and Amazon MQ REST APIs, and then plan to migrate to Amazon MQ.

Amazon MQ Tutorials

The following tutorials show how you can work with Amazon MQ and ActiveMQ using the AWS Management Console and Java. To use the example code, you must install the Java Standard Edition Development Kit and make some changes to the code.

- Creating and Configuring a Broker
- Creating and Applying Broker Configurations
- Editing and Managing Broker Configurations
- Connecting a Java Application to Your Broker
- Listing Brokers and Viewing Broker Details
- Creating and Managing Amazon MQ Broker Users
- Rebooting a Broker
- Deleting a Broker
- Accessing CloudWatch Metrics for Amazon MQ

Tutorial: Creating and Configuring an Amazon MQ Broker

A *broker* is a message broker environment running on Amazon MQ. It is the basic building block of Amazon MQ. The combined description of the broker instance *class* (`m4`, `t2`) and *size* (`large`, `micro`) is a *broker instance type* (for example, `mq.m4.large`). For more information, see Broker.

The first and most common Amazon MQ task is creating a broker. The following example shows how you can use the AWS Management Console to create and configure a broker using the AWS Management Console.

- Step 1: Configure basic broker settings
- Step 2: (Optional) Configure advanced broker settings
- Step 3: Finish creating the broker

Step 1: Configure basic broker settings

1. Sign in to the Amazon MQ console.

2. Do one of the following:

   - If this is your first time using Amazon MQ, in the **Create a broker** section, type `MyBroker` for **Broker name** and then choose **Next step**.

   - If you have created a broker before, on the **Create a broker** page, in the **Broker details** section, type `MyBroker` for **Broker name**.

3. Choose a **Broker instance type** (for example, **mq.m4.large**). For more information, see Instance Types.

4. Choose a **Deployment mode**:

   - A **Single-instance broker** is comprised of one broker in one Availability Zone. The broker communicates with your application and with an AWS storage location. For more information, see Amazon MQ Single-Instance Broker.

   - An **Active/standby broker for high availability** is comprised of two brokers in two different Availability Zones, configured in a *redundant pair*. These brokers communicate synchronously with your application, and with a shared storage location. For more information, see Amazon MQ Active/Standby Broker for High Availability. **Note**
   Currently, Amazon MQ supports only the `ActiveMQ` broker engine, version `5.15.0`.

5. In the **ActiveMQ Web Console access** section, type a **Username** and **Password**.

Step 2: (Optional) Configure advanced broker settings

Important
Subnet(s) – A single-instance broker requires one subnet (for example, the default subnet). An active/standby broker for high availability requires two subnets. **Security group(s)** – Both single-instance brokers and active/standby brokers for high availability require at least one security group (for example, the default security group). **VPC** – A broker's subnet(s) and security group(s) must be in the same VPC. EC2-Classic resources aren't supported. **Public accessibility** – Disabling public accessibility makes the broker accessible only within your VPC. For more information, see Prefer Brokers without Public Accessibility.

1. Expand the **Advanced settings** section.

2. In the **Configuration** section, choose **Create a new configuration with default values** or **Select an existing configuration**. For more information, see Configuration and Amazon MQ Broker Configuration Parameters.

3. In the **Network and security section**, configure your broker's connectivity:

1. Select the default **Virtual Private Cloud (VPC)** or create a new one on the Amazon VPC console. For more information, see What is Amazon VPC? in the *Amazon VPC User Guide*.

2. Select the default **Subnets** or create new ones on the Amazon VPC console. For more information, see VPCs and Subnets in the *Amazon VPC User Guide*.

3. Select your **Security group(s)**.

4. Choose the **Public accessibility** of your broker.

4. In the **Maintenance section**, configure your broker's maintenance schedule:

1. To upgrade the broker to new versions as Apache releases them, choose **Enable automatic minor version upgrades**. Automatic upgrades occur during the 2-hour *maintenance window* defined by the day of the week, the time of day (in 24-hour format), and the time zone (UTC by default). **Note** For an active/standby broker for high availability, if one of the broker instances undergoes maintenance, it takes Amazon MQ a short while to take the inactive instance out of service, allowing the healthy standby instance to become active and to begin accepting incoming communications.

2. Do one of the following:

   - To allow Amazon MQ to select the maintenance window automatically, choose **No preference**.

   - To set a custom maintenance window, choose **Select maintenance window** and then specify the **Start day** and **Start time** of the upgrades.

Step 3: Finish creating the broker

1. Choose **Create broker**.

   While Amazon MQ creates your broker, it displays the **Creation in progress** status.

   Creating the broker takes about 15 minutes.

   When your broker is created successfully, Amazon MQ displays the **Running** status.

Name	Status	Deployment mode	Instance type
MyBroker	Running	Single-instance broker	mq.m4.large

2. Choose *MyBroker*.

   On the *MyBroker* page, in the **Connect** section, note your broker's **ActiveMQ Web Console** URL, for example:

   ```
   1  https://b-1234a5b6-78cd-901e-2fgh-3i45j6k17819-1.mq.us-east-2.amazonaws.com:8162
   ```

   Also, note your broker's wire-level protocol **Endpoints**. The following is an example of an OpenWire endpoint:

   ```
   1  ssl://b-1234a5b6-78cd-901e-2fgh-3i45j6k17819-1.mq.us-east-2.amazonaws.com:61617
   ```

Note
For an active/standby broker for high availability, Amazon MQ provides two ActiveMQ Web Console URLs, but only one URL is active at a time. Likewise, Amazon MQ provides two endpoints for each wire-level protocol, but only one endpoint is active in each pair at a time. The -1 and -2 suffixes denote a redundant pair. For more information, see Amazon MQ Broker Architecture).
For wire-level protocol endpoints, you can allow your application to connect to either endpoint by using the Failover Transport.

Tutorial: Creating and Applying Amazon MQ Broker Configurations

A *configuration* contains all of the settings for your ActiveMQ broker, in XML format (similar to ActiveMQ's `activemq.xml` file). You can create a configuration before creating any brokers. You can then apply the configuration to one or more brokers. You can apply a configuration immediately or during a 2-hour *maintenance window*.

Note
For an active/standby broker for high availability, if one of the broker instances undergoes maintenance, it takes Amazon MQ a short while to take the inactive instance out of service, allowing the healthy standby instance to become active and to begin accepting incoming communications.

For more information, see the following:

- Configuration
- Amazon MQ Broker Configuration Lifecycle
- Amazon MQ Broker Configuration Parameters
- Tutorial: Editing Amazon MQ Broker Configurations and Managing Configuration Revisions

The following example shows how you can create and apply an Amazon MQ broker configuration using the AWS Management Console.

- Step 1: Create a configuration from scratch
- Step 2: Create a new configuration revision
- Step 3: Apply a configuration revision to your broker

Step 1: Create a configuration from scratch

1. Sign in to the Amazon MQ console.

2. On the left, expand the navigation panel and choose **Configurations**.

3. On the **Configurations** page, choose **Create configuration**.

4. On the **Create configuration** page, in the **Details** section, type the **Configuration name** (for example, `MyConfiguration`). **Note**
   Currently, Amazon MQ supports only the `ActiveMQ` broker engine, version `5.15.0`.

5. Choose **Create configuration**.

Step 2: Create a new configuration revision

1. From the configuration list, choose *MyConfiguration*. **Note**
   The first configuration revision is always created for you when Amazon MQ creates the configuration.

On the *MyConfiguration* page, the broker engine type and version that your new configuration revision uses (for example, **Apache ActiveMQ 5.15.0**) are displayed.

2. On the **Configuration details** tab, the configuration revision number, description, and broker configuration in XML format are displayed. **Note**
Editing the current configuration creates a new configuration revision.

Revision 1 Auto-generated default for MyBroker-configuration on ActiveMQ 5.15.0 `Latest`

Amazon MQ configurations support a limited subset of ActiveMQ properties. Info

```
1  <?xml version="1.0" encoding="UTF-8" standalone="yes"?>
2  <broker xmlns="http://activemq.apache.org/schema/core">
3    <!--
4    A configuration contains all of the settings for your ActiveMQ broker, in XML format
   (similar to ActiveMQ's activemq.xml file).
5     You can create a configuration before creating any brokers. You can then apply the
   configuration to one or more brokers.
```

3. Choose **Edit configuration** and make changes to the XML configuration.

4. Choose **Save**.

   The **Save revisions** dialog box is displayed.

5. (Optional) Type **A description of the changes in this revision**.

6. Choose **Save**.

   The new revision of the configuration is saved. **Important**
   The Amazon MQ console automatically sanitizes invalid and prohibited configuration parameters according to a schema. For more information and a full list of permitted XML parameters, see Amazon MQ Broker Configuration Parameters.
   Making changes to a configuration does *not* apply the changes to the broker immediately. To apply your changes, you must wait for the next 2-hour maintenance window or reboot the broker. For more information, see Amazon MQ Broker Configuration Lifecycle.
   Currently, it isn't possible to delete a configuration.

Step 3: Apply a configuration revision to your broker

1. On the left, expand the navigation panel and choose **Brokers**.

Amazon MQ ✕

Brokers

Configurations

2. From the broker list, select your broker (for example, **MyBroker**) and then choose **Edit**.

3. On the **Edit** *MyBroker* page, in the **Configuration** section, select a **Configuration** **1** and a **Revision** **2** and then choose **Schedule Modifications** **3** .

4. In the **Schedule broker modifications** section, choose whether to apply modifications **During the next scheduled maintenance window** or **Immediately**. **Important**
Your broker will be offline while it is being rebooted.

5. Choose **Apply**.

   Your configuration revision is applied to your broker at the specified time.

Tutorial: Editing Amazon MQ Broker Configurations and Managing Configuration Revisions

A *configuration* contains all of the settings for your ActiveMQ broker, in XML format (similar to ActiveMQ's `activemq.xml` file). You can apply a configuration immediately or during a 2-hour *maintenance window*.

Note
For an active/standby broker for high availability, if one of the broker instances undergoes maintenance, it takes Amazon MQ a short while to take the inactive instance out of service, allowing the healthy standby instance to become active and to begin accepting incoming communications.

To keep track of the changes you make to your configuration, you can create *configuration revisions*.

For more information, see the following:

- Configuration
- Amazon MQ Broker Configuration Lifecycle
- Amazon MQ Broker Configuration Parameters
- Tutorial: Creating and Applying Amazon MQ Broker Configurations

The following examples show how you can edit Amazon MQ broker configurations and manage broker configuration revisions using the AWS Management Console.

- To view a previous configuration revision
- To edit the current configuration revision
- To apply a configuration revision to your broker
- To roll back your broker to the last configuration revision

To view a previous configuration revision

1. Sign in to the Amazon MQ console.

2. From the broker list, select your broker (for example, **MyBroker**) and then choose **Edit**.

3. On the **Edit** *MyBroker* page, in the **Configuration** section, select a **Configuration** ❶ and a **Revision** ❷ and then choose **View** ❸.

Note
Unless you select a configuration when you create a broker, the first configuration revision is always created for you when Amazon MQ creates the broker.

On the *MyBroker* page, the broker engine type and version that the configuration uses (for example, **Apache ActiveMQ 5.15.0**) are displayed.

4. Choose **Revision history**.

5. The configuration **Revision** number, **Revision date**, and **Description** are displayed for each revision.

6. Select a revision and choose **View details**.

The broker configuration in XML format is displayed.

To edit the current configuration revision

1. Sign in to the Amazon MQ console.

2. From the broker list, select your broker (for example, **MyBroker**) and then choose **Edit**.

3. On the *MyBroker* page, choose **Edit**.

4. On the **Edit** *MyBroker* page, in the **Configuration** section, select a **Configuration** ① and a **Revision** ② and then choose **View** ③.

Note
Unless you select a configuration when you create a broker, the first configuration revision is always created for you when Amazon MQ creates the broker.

On the *MyBroker* page, the broker engine type and version that the configuration uses (for example, **Apache ActiveMQ 5.15.0**) are displayed.

5. On the **Configuration details** tab, the configuration revision number, description, and broker configuration in XML format are displayed. **Note**
Editing the current configuration creates a new configuration revision.

Revision 1 Auto-generated default for MyBroker-configuration on ActiveMQ 5.15.0 `Latest`

Amazon MQ configurations support a limited subset of ActiveMQ properties. Info

```
1  <?xml version="1.0" encoding="UTF-8" standalone="yes"?>
2  <broker xmlns="http://activemq.apache.org/schema/core">
3    <!--
4    A configuration contains all of the settings for your ActiveMQ broker, in XML format
    (similar to ActiveMQ's activemq.xml file).
5    You can create a configuration before creating any brokers. You can then apply the
    configuration to one or more brokers.
```

6. Choose **Edit configuration** and make changes to the XML configuration.

7. Choose **Save**.

The **Save revisions** dialog box is displayed.

8. (Optional) Type **A description of the changes in this revision**.

9. Choose **Save**.

The new revision of the configuration is saved. **Important**
The Amazon MQ console automatically sanitizes invalid and prohibited configuration parameters according to a schema. For more information and a full list of permitted XML parameters, see Amazon MQ Broker Configuration Parameters.

Making changes to a configuration does *not* apply the changes to the broker immediately. To apply your changes, you must wait for the next 2-hour maintenance window or reboot the broker. For more information, see Amazon MQ Broker Configuration Lifecycle.

Currently, it isn't possible to delete a configuration.

To apply a configuration revision to your broker

1. Sign in to the Amazon MQ console.

2. From the broker list, select your broker (for example, **MyBroker**) and then choose **Edit**.

3. On the **Edit** *MyBroker* page, in the **Configuration** section, select a **Configuration** ❶ and a **Revision** ❷ and then choose **Schedule Modifications** ❸.

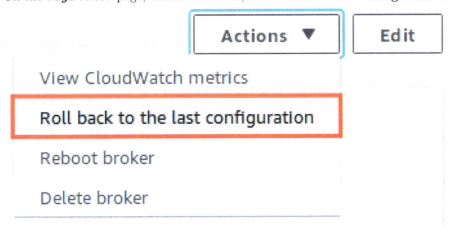

4. In the **Schedule broker modifications** section, choose whether to apply modifications **During the next scheduled maintenance window** or **Immediately**. **Important** Your broker will be offline while it is being rebooted.

5. Choose **Apply**.

   Your configuration revision is applied to your broker at the specified time.

To roll back your broker to the last configuration revision

1. Sign in to the Amazon MQ console.

2. From the broker list, choose the name of your broker (for example, **MyBroker**).

3. On the *MyBroker* page, choose **Actions**, **Roll back to last configuration**.

4. (Optional) To review the **Current configuration** or the **Last configuration**, on the **Roll back to the last configuration** page, in the **Summary** section, choose **View** for either configuration.

5. In the **Schedule broker modifications** section, choose whether to apply modifications **During the next scheduled maintenance window** or **Immediately. Important** Your broker will be offline while it is being rebooted.

6. Choose **Apply**.

   Your configuration revision is applied to your broker at the specified time.

Tutorial: Connecting a Java Application to Your Amazon MQ Broker

After you create an Amazon MQ broker, you can connect your application to it. The following examples show how you can use the Java Message Service (JMS) to create a connection to the broker, create a queue, and send a message. For a complete, working Java example, see Working Examples of Using Java Message Service (JMS) with ActiveMQ.

You can connect to ActiveMQ brokers using various ActiveMQ clients. We recommend using the ActiveMQ Client.

Important
To ensure that your broker is accessible within your VPC, you must enable the `enableDnsHostnames` and `enableDnsSupport` VPC attributes. For more information, see DNS Support in your VPC in the *Amazon VPC User Guide*.

- Prerequisites
- To create a message producer and send a message
- To create a message consumer and receive the message

Prerequisites

Enable Inbound Connections

1. Sign in to the Amazon MQ console.

2. From the broker list, choose the name of your broker (for example, **MyBroker**).

3. On the *MyBroker* page, in the **Connections** section, note the addresses and ports of the broker's ActiveMQ Web Console URL and wire-level protocols.

4. In the **Details** section, under **Security and network**, choose the name of your security group or ↗.

   The **Security Groups** page of the EC2 Dashboard is displayed.

5. From the security group list, choose your security group.

6. At the bottom of the page, choose **Inbound**, and then choose **Edit**.

7. In the **Edit inbound rules** dialog box, add a rule for every URL or endpoint that you want to be publicly accessible (the following example shows how to do this for an ActiveMQ Web Console).

   1. Choose **Add Rule**.

   2. For **Type**, select **Custom TCP**.

   3. For **Port Range**, type the ActiveMQ Web Console port (`8162`).

   4. For **Source**, leave **Custom** selected and then type the IP address of the system that you want to be able to access the ActiveMQ Web Console (for example, `192.0.2.1`).

   5. Choose **Save**.

      Your broker can now accept inbound connections.

Add Java Dependencies

Add the `activemq-client.jar` and `activemq-pool.jar` packages to your Java class path. The following example shows these dependencies in a Maven project `pom.xml` file.

```
1 <dependencies>
2     <dependency>
3         <groupId>org.apache.activemq</groupId>
4         <artifactId>activemq-client</artifactId>
5         <version>5.15.0</version>
6     </dependency>
7     <dependency>
8         <groupId>org.apache.activemq</groupId>
9         <artifactId>activemq-pool</artifactId>
10         <version>5.15.0</version>
11     </dependency>
12 </dependencies>
```

For more information about `activemq-client.jar`, see Initial Configuration in the Apache ActiveMQ documentation.

To create a message producer and send a message

1. Create a JMS pooled connection factory for the message producer using your broker's endpoint and then call the `createConnection` method against the factory. **Note**
   For an active/standby broker for high availability, Amazon MQ provides two ActiveMQ Web Console URLs, but only one URL is active at a time. Likewise, Amazon MQ provides two endpoints for each wire-level protocol, but only one endpoint is active in each pair at a time. The −1 and −2 suffixes denote a redundant pair. For more information, see Amazon MQ Broker Architecture).
   For wire-level protocol endpoints, you can allow your application to connect to either endpoint by using the Failover Transport.

```
1 // Create a connection factory.
2 final ActiveMQConnectionFactory connectionFactory = new ActiveMQConnectionFactory(
      wireLevelEndpoint);
3
4 // Pass the username and password.
5 connectionFactory.setUserName(activeMqUsername);
6 connectionFactory.setPassword(activeMqPassword);
7
8 // Create a pooled connection factory.
9 final PooledConnectionFactory pooledConnectionFactory = new PooledConnectionFactory();
10 pooledConnectionFactory.setConnectionFactory(connectionFactory);
11 pooledConnectionFactory.setMaxConnections(10);
12
13 // Establish a connection for the producer.
14 final Connection producerConnection = pooledConnectionFactory.createConnection();
15 producerConnection.start();
```

Note
Message producers should always use the `PooledConnectionFactory` class. For more information, see Always Use Connection Pooling.

1. Create a session, a queue named `MyQueue`, and a message producer.

```
1 // Create a session.
2 final Session producerSession = producerConnection.createSession(false, Session.
      AUTO_ACKNOWLEDGE);
3
4 // Create a queue named "MyQueue".
```

```
5 final Destination producerDestination = producerSession.createQueue("MyQueue");
6
7 // Create a producer from the session to the queue.
8 final MessageProducer producer = producerSession.createProducer(producerDestination);
9 producer.setDeliveryMode(DeliveryMode.NON_PERSISTENT);
```

2. Create the message string `"Hello from Amazon MQ!"` and then send the message.

```
1 // Create a message.
2 final String text = "Hello from Amazon MQ!";
3 TextMessage producerMessage = producerSession.createTextMessage(text);
4
5 // Send the message.
6 producer.send(producerMessage);
7 System.out.println("Message sent.");
```

3. Clean up the producer.

```
1 producer.close();
2 producerSession.close();
3 producerConnection.close();
```

To create a message consumer and receive the message

1. Create a JMS connection factory for the message producer using your broker's endpoint and then call the `createConnection` method against the factory.

```
1 // Create a connection factory.
2 final ActiveMQConnectionFactory connectionFactory = new ActiveMQConnectionFactory(
    wireLevelEndpoint);
3
4 // Pass the username and password.
5 connectionFactory.setUserName(activeMqUsername);
6 connectionFactory.setPassword(activeMqPassword);
7
8 // Establish a connection for the consumer.
9 final Connection consumerConnection = connectionFactory.createConnection();
10 consumerConnection.start();
```

Note
Message consumers should *never* use the `PooledConnectionFactory` class. For more information, see Always Use Connection Pooling.

1. Create a session, a queue named `MyQueue`, and a message consumer.

```
1 // Create a session.
2 final Session consumerSession = consumerConnection.createSession(false, Session.
    AUTO_ACKNOWLEDGE);
3
4 // Create a queue named "MyQueue".
5 final Destination consumerDestination = consumerSession.createQueue("MyQueue");
6
7 // Create a message consumer from the session to the queue.
8 final MessageConsumer consumer = consumerSession.createConsumer(consumerDestination);
```

2. Begin to wait for messages and receive the message when it arrives.

```
1 // Begin to wait for messages.
2 final Message consumerMessage = consumer.receive(1000);
3
4 // Receive the message when it arrives.
5 final TextMessage consumerTextMessage = (TextMessage) consumerMessage;
6 System.out.println("Message received: " + consumerTextMessage.getText());
```

Note

Unlike AWS messaging services (such as Amazon SQS), the consumer is constantly connected to the broker.

1. Close the consumer, session, and connection.

```
1 consumer.close();
2 consumerSession.close();
3 consumerConnection.close();
4 pooledConnectionFactory.stop();
```

Tutorial: Listing Amazon MQ Brokers and Viewing Broker Details

When you request that Amazon MQ create a broker, the creation process can take about 15 minutes..

The following example shows how you can confirm your broker's existence by listing your brokers in the current region using the AWS Management Console.

To list brokers and view broker details

1. Sign in to the Amazon MQ console.

   Your brokers in the current region are listed.

Name	Status	Deployment mode	Instance type
○ MyBroker	Running	Single-instance broker	mq.m4.large
○ MyBroker2	Running	Active/standby broker for high availability	mq.m4.large

   The following information is displayed for each broker:

   - **Name**
   - **Creation** date
   - **Status**
   - **Deployment mode**
   - **Instance type**

2. Choose your broker's name (for example, **MyBroker**).

   On the *MyBroker* page, the configured **Details** are displayed for your broker:

Details

ARN Info

arn:aws:mq:us-east-1:⬛⬛⬛⬛⬛:broker:MyBroker:b-⬛⬛⬛⬛-32ef-4f18-b089-4dda943e9aa1

Specifications

Broker status

Running

Broker name

MyBroker

Broker instance type Info

mq.m4.large

Deployment mode Info

Single-instance broker

Broker engine Info

ActiveMQ

Broker engine version

5.15.0

Configuration

Configuration name

MyBroker-configuration

Configuration revision

Revision 1 - Auto-generated default for MyBroker-configuration on ActiveMQ 5.15.0

Security and network

VPC Info

vpc-⬛⬛⬛ ↗

Subnet(s) Info

subnet-⬛⬛⬛ ↗

Security group(s) Info

sg-⬛⬛⬛ ↗

Public accessibility Info

Yes

Maintenance

Automatic minor version upgrade

Yes

Maintenance window

Monday 01:00 - 03:00

Next: 12/04/2017

Below the **Details** section, the following information is displayed:

- In the **Connections** section, the ActiveMQ Web Console URL and the wire-level protocol endpoints
- In the **Users** section, the users associated with the broker

Tutorial: Creating and Managing Amazon MQ Broker Users

An ActiveMQ *user* is a person or an application that can access the queues and topics of an ActiveMQ broker. You can configure users to have specific permissions. For example, you can allow some users to access the ActiveMQ Web Console.

A user can belong to a *group*. You can configure which users belong to which groups and which groups have permission to send to, receive from, and administer specific queues and topics.

The following examples show how you can create, edit, and delete Amazon MQ broker users using the AWS Management Console.

- To create a new user
- To edit an existing user
- To delete a existing user

To create a new user

1. Sign in to the Amazon MQ console.

2. From the broker list, choose the name of your broker (for example, **MyBroker**) and then choose **Edit**.

   On the *MyBroker* page, in the **Users** section, all the users for this broker are listed.

Username	Console access	Groups	Pending modifications
paolo.santos	No	Devs	
jane.doe	Yes	Admins	

3. Choose **Create user**.

4. In the **Create user** dialog box, type a **Username** and **Password**.

5. (Optional) Type the names of groups to which the user belongs, separated by commas (for example: `Devs, Admins`).

6. (Optional) To enable the user to access the ActiveMQ Web Console, choose **ActiveMQ Web Console**.

7. Choose **Create user**. **Important**
   Making changes to a user does *not* apply the changes to the user immediately. To apply your changes, you must wait for the next 2-hour maintenance window or reboot the broker. For more information, see Amazon MQ Broker Configuration Lifecycle.

To edit an existing user

1. Sign in to the Amazon MQ console.

2. From the broker list, choose the name of your broker (for example, **MyBroker**) and then choose **Edit**.

   On the *MyBroker* page, in the **Users** section, all the users for this broker are listed.

Username	Console access	Groups	Pending modifications
paolo.santos	No	Devs	
jane.doe	Yes	Admins	

3. Select a username and choose **Edit**.

   The **Edit user** dialog box is displayed.

4. (Optional) Type a new **Password**.

5. (Optional) Add or remove the names of groups to which the user belongs, separated by commas (for example: `Managers, Admins`).

6. (Optional) To enable the user to access the ActiveMQ Web Console, choose **ActiveMQ Web Console**.

7. To save the changes to the user, choose **Done. Important**
   Making changes to a user does *not* apply the changes to the user immediately. To apply your changes, you must wait for the next 2-hour maintenance window or reboot the broker. For more information, see Amazon MQ Broker Configuration Lifecycle.

To delete a existing user

1. Sign in to the Amazon MQ console.

2. From the broker list, choose the name of your broker (for example, **MyBroker**) and then choose **Edit**.

   On the *MyBroker* page, in the **Users** section, all the users for this broker are listed.

Username	Console access	Groups	Pending modifications
paolo.santos	No	Devs	
jane.doe	Yes	Admins	

3. Select a username (for example, *MyUser*) and then choose **Delete**.

4. To confirm deleting the user, in the **Delete *MyUser*?** dialog box, choose **Delete. Important**
   Making changes to a user does *not* apply the changes to the user immediately. To apply your changes, you must wait for the next 2-hour maintenance window or reboot the broker. For more information, see Amazon MQ Broker Configuration Lifecycle.

Tutorial: Rebooting an Amazon MQ Broker

To apply a new configuration to a broker, you can reboot the broker. In addition, if your broker becomes unresponsive, you can reboot it to recover from a faulty state.

The following example shows how you can reboot an Amazon MQ broker using the AWS Management Console.

To reboot an Amazon MQ broker

1. Sign in to the Amazon MQ console.

2. From the broker list, choose the name of your broker (for example, **MyBroker**).

3. On the *MyBroker* page, choose **Actions**, **Reboot broker. Important**
   Your broker will be offline while it is being rebooted.

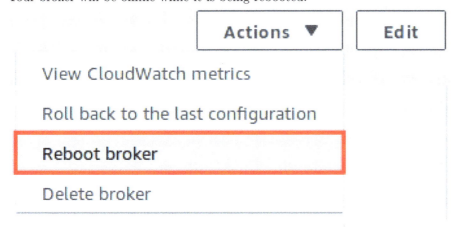

4. In the **Reboot broker** dialog box, choose **Reboot**.

   Rebooting the broker takes about 5 minutes.

Tutorial: Deleting an Amazon MQ Broker

If you don't use an Amazon MQ broker (and don't foresee using it in the near future), it is a best practice to delete it from Amazon MQ to reduce your AWS costs.

The following example shows how you can delete a broker using the AWS Management Console.

To delete an Amazon MQ broker

1. Sign in to the Amazon MQ console.

2. From the broker list, select your broker (for example, **MyBroker**) and then choose **Delete**.

3. In the **Delete *MyBroker*?** dialog box, type `delete` and then choose **Delete**.

   Deleting a broker takes about 5 minutes.

Tutorial: Accessing CloudWatch Metrics for Amazon MQ

Amazon MQ and Amazon CloudWatch are integrated so you can use CloudWatch to view and analyze metrics for your ActiveMQ broker and the broker's destinations (queues and topics). You can view and analyze your Amazon MQ metrics from the CloudWatch console, the AWS CLI, or the CloudWatch CLI. CloudWatch metrics for Amazon MQ are automatically polled from the broker and then pushed to CloudWatch every minute.

For a full list of Amazon MQ metrics, see Monitoring Amazon MQ using Amazon CloudWatch.

For information about creating a CloudWatch alarm for a metrics, see Create or Edit a CloudWatch Alarm in the *Amazon CloudWatch User Guide.*

Note
There is no charge for the Amazon MQ metrics reported in CloudWatch. These metrics are provided as part of the Amazon MQ service.
CloudWatch monitors only the first 200 destinations.

- AWS Management Console
- AWS Command Line Interface
- Amazon CloudWatch API

AWS Management Console

The following example shows you how to access CloudWatch metrics for Amazon MQ using the AWS Management Console.

Note
If you're already signed into the Amazon MQ console, on the broker **Details** page, choose **Actions**, **View CloudWatch metrics**.

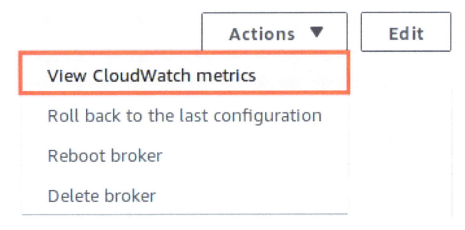

1. Sign in to the CloudWatch console.

2. On the navigation panel, choose **Metrics**.

3. Select the **AmazonMQ** metric namespace.

4. Select one of the following metric dimensions:

- **Broker Metrics**
- **Queue Metrics by Broker**
- **Topic Metrics by Broker**

In this example, **Broker Metrics** is selected.

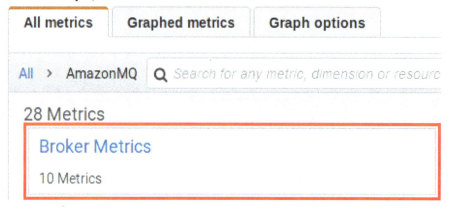

5. You can now examine your Amazon MQ metrics:

- To sort the metrics, use the column heading.
- To graph the metric, select the check box next to the metric.
- To filter by metric, choose the metric name and then choose **Add to search**.

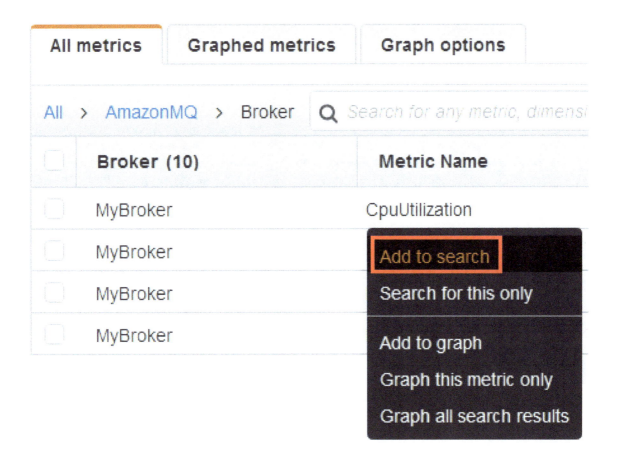

AWS Command Line Interface

To access Amazon MQ metrics using the AWS CLI, use the `[get\-metric\-statistics](http://docs.aws.amazon.com/cli/latest/reference/cloudwatch/get-metric-statistics.html)` command.

For more information, see Get Statistics for a Metric in the *Amazon CloudWatch User Guide*.

Amazon CloudWatch API

To access Amazon MQ metrics using the CloudWatch API, use the `[GetMetricStatistics](http://docs.aws.amazon.com/AmazonCloudWatch/latest/APIReference/API_GetMetricStatistics.html)` action.

For more information, see Get Statistics for a Metric in the *Amazon CloudWatch User Guide*.

How Amazon MQ Works

Amazon MQ makes it easy to create a message broker with the computing and storage resources that fit your needs. You can create, manage, and delete brokers using the AWS Management Console, Amazon MQ REST API, or the AWS Command Line Interface.

This section describes the basic elements of a message broker, lists available Amazon MQ broker instance types and their statuses, provides an overview of broker architecture, explains broker configuration parameters and offers a working example of using Java Message Service (JMS) with an ActiveMQ broker.

To learn about Amazon MQ REST APIs, see the *Amazon MQ REST API Reference.*

- Amazon MQ Basic Elements
- Amazon MQ Broker Architecture
- Amazon MQ Broker Configuration Parameters
- Working Java Example

Amazon MQ Basic Elements

This section introduces key concepts essential to understanding Amazon MQ.

- Broker
- Configuration
- Engine
- User

Broker

A *broker* is a message broker environment running on Amazon MQ. It is the basic building block of Amazon MQ. The combined description of the broker instance *class* (`m4`, `t2`) and *size* (`large`, `micro`) is a *broker instance type* (for example, `mq.m4.large`). For more information, see Instance Types.

- A *single-instance broker* is comprised of one broker in one Availability Zone. The broker communicates with your application and with an AWS storage location.

- An *active/standby broker for high availability* is comprised of two brokers in two different Availability Zones, configured in a *redundant pair*. These brokers communicate synchronously with your application, and with a shared storage location.

For more information, see Amazon MQ Broker Architecture.

You can enable *automatic minor version upgrades* to new minor versions of the broker engine, as Apache releases new versions. Automatic upgrades occur during the 2-hour *maintenance window* defined by the day of the week, the time of day (in 24-hour format), and the time zone (UTC by default).

For information about creating and managing brokers, see the following:

- Tutorial: Creating and Configuring an Amazon MQ Broker

- Brokers

- Statuses

Attributes

A broker has several attributes, for example:

- A name (`MyBroker`)

- An ID (`b-1234a5b6-78cd-901e-2fgh-3i45j6k17819`)

- An Amazon Resource Name (ARN) (`arn:aws:mq:us-east-2:123456789012:broker:MyBroker:b-1234a5b6-78cd-901e-2fgh-3i45j6k17819`)

- An ActiveMQ Web Console URL (`https://b-1234a5b6-78cd-901e-2fgh-3i45j6k17819-1.mq.us-east-2.amazonaws.com:8162`)

  For more information, see Web Console in the Apache ActiveMQ documentation. **Important**
  If you specify an authorization map which doesn't include the `activemq-webconsole` group, you won't be able to use the ActiveMQ Web Console because the group isn't authorized to send messages to, or receive messages from, the Amazon MQ broker.

- Wire-level protocol endpoints:

  - `amqp+ssl://b-1234a5b6-78cd-901e-2fgh-3i45j6k17819-1.mq.us-east-2.amazonaws.com:5671`

  - `mqtt+ssl://b-1234a5b6-78cd-901e-2fgh-3i45j6k17819-1.mq.us-east-2.amazonaws.com:8883`

  - `ssl://b-1234a5b6-78cd-901e-2fgh-3i45j6k17819-1.mq.us-east-2.amazonaws.com:61617`
    Note
    This is an OpenWire endpoint.

  - `stomp+ssl://b-1234a5b6-78cd-901e-2fgh-3i45j6k17819-1.mq.us-east-2.amazonaws.com:61614`

  - `wss://b-1234a5b6-78cd-901e-2fgh-3i45j6k17819-1.mq.us-east-2.amazonaws.com:61619`

For more information, see Configuring Transports in the Apache ActiveMQ documentation.

Note

For an active/standby broker for high availability, Amazon MQ provides two ActiveMQ Web Console URLs, but only one URL is active at a time. Likewise, Amazon MQ provides two endpoints for each wire-level protocol, but only one endpoint is active in each pair at a time. The -1 and -2 suffixes denote a redundant pair.

For a full list of broker attributes, see the following in the *Amazon MQ REST API Reference*:

- REST Operation ID: Broker
- REST Operation ID: Brokers
- REST Operation ID: Broker Reboot

Instance Types

The combined description of the broker instance *class* (m4, t2) and *size* (large, micro) is a *broker instance type* (for example, mq.m4.large). The following table lists the available Amazon MQ broker instance types.

Instance Type	vCPU	Memory (GiB)	Network Performance
Standard			
mq.m4.large	2	8	Moderate
Micro-Instance			
mq.t2.micro	1	1	Low

Note

The mq.t2.micro instance type (single-instance brokers only) qualifies for the AWS Free Tier.
Using the mq.t2.micro instance type is subject to * CPU credits and baseline performance*—with the ability to *burst* above the baseline level. If your application requires *fixed performance*, consider using an mq.m4.large instance type.

Statuses

A broker's current condition is indicated by a *status*. The following table lists the statuses of an Amazon MQ broker.

Console	API	Description
Creation failed	CREATION_FAILED	The broker couldn't be created.
Creation in progress	CRE-ATION_IN_PROGRESS	The broker is currently being created.
Deletion in progress	DELE-TION_IN_PROGRESS	The broker is currently being deleted.
Reboot in progress	REBOOT_IN_PROGRESS	The broker is currently being rebooted.
Running	RUNNING	The broker is operational.

Configuration

A *configuration* contains all of the settings for your ActiveMQ broker, in XML format (similar to ActiveMQ's `activemq.xml` file). You can create a configuration before creating any brokers. You can then apply the configuration to one or more brokers.

Important
Making changes to a configuration does *not* apply the changes to the broker immediately. To apply your changes, you must wait for the next 2-hour maintenance window or reboot the broker. For more information, see Amazon MQ Broker Configuration Lifecycle.
Currently, it isn't possible to delete a configuration.

For information about creating, editing, and managing configurations, see the following:

- Tutorial: Creating and Applying Amazon MQ Broker Configurations

- Tutorial: Editing Amazon MQ Broker Configurations and Managing Configuration Revisions

- Configurations

- Amazon MQ Broker Configuration Parameters

To keep track of the changes you make to your configuration, you can create *configuration revisions*. For more information, see Tutorial: Creating and Applying Amazon MQ Broker Configurations and Tutorial: Editing Amazon MQ Broker Configurations and Managing Configuration Revisions.

Attributes

A broker configuration has several attributes, for example:

- A name (`MyConfiguration`)

- An ID (`c-1234a5b6-78cd-901e-2fgh-3i45j6k17819`)

- An Amazon Resource Name (ARN) (`arn:aws:mq:us-east-2:123456789012:configuration:MyConfiguration:c-1234a5b6-78cd-901e-2fgh-3i45j6k17819`)

For a full list of configuration attributes, see the following in the *Amazon MQ REST API Reference*:

- REST Operation ID: Configuration

- REST Operation ID: Configurations

For a full list of configuration revision attributes, see the following:

- REST Operation ID: Configuration Revision

- REST Operation ID: Configuration Revisions

Engine

A *broker engine* is a type of message broker that runs on Amazon MQ.

Note
Currently, Amazon MQ supports only the `ActiveMQ` broker engine, version `5.15.0`.

User

An ActiveMQ *user* is a person or an application that can access the queues and topics of an ActiveMQ broker. You can configure users to have specific permissions. For example, you can allow some users to access the ActiveMQ Web Console.

A user can belong to a *group*. You can configure which users belong to which groups and which groups have permission to send to, receive from, and administer specific queues and topics.

Important
Making changes to a user does *not* apply the changes to the user immediately. To apply your changes, you must wait for the next 2-hour maintenance window or reboot the broker. For more information, see Amazon MQ Broker Configuration Lifecycle.

For information about users and groups, see the following in the Apache ActiveMQ documentation:

- Authorization
- Authorization Example

For information about creating, editing, and deleting ActiveMQ users, see the following:

- Tutorial: Creating and Managing Amazon MQ Broker Users
- Users

Attributes

For a full list of user attributes, see the following in the *Amazon MQ REST API Reference*:

- REST Operation ID: User
- REST Operation ID: Users

Amazon MQ Broker Architecture

Amazon MQ brokers can be created as *single-instance brokers* or *active/standby brokers for high availability*. For both deployment modes, Amazon MQ provides high durability by storing its data redundantly, across multiple Availability Zones (multi-AZs) within an AWS Region. Amazon MQ ensures high availability by providing failover to a standby instance in a second Availability Zone.

Note
Amazon MQ uses Apache KahaDB as its data store. Other data stores, such as JDBC and LevelDB, aren't supported.

- Amazon MQ Single-Instance Broker
- Amazon MQ Active/Standby Broker for High Availability
- Amazon MQ Broker Configuration Lifecycle

Amazon MQ Single-Instance Broker

A *single-instance broker* is comprised of one broker in one Availability Zone. The broker communicates with your application and with an AWS storage location.

The following diagram illustrates a single-instance broker.

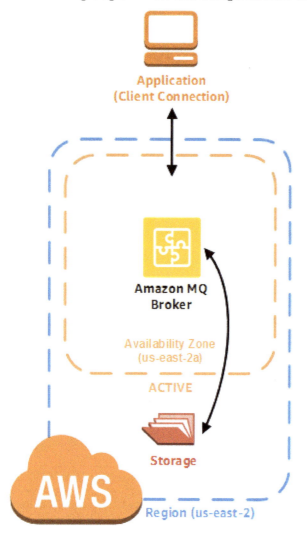

Amazon MQ Active/Standby Broker for High Availability

An *active/standby broker for high availability* is comprised of two brokers in two different Availability Zones, configured in a *redundant pair*. These brokers communicate synchronously with your application, and with a shared storage location.

Normally, only one of the broker instances is active at any time, while the other broker instance is on standby. If one of the broker instances malfunctions or undergoes maintenance, it takes Amazon MQ a short while to take the inactive instance out of service, allowing the healthy standby instance to become active and to begin accepting incoming communications. When you reboot a broker, the failover takes only a few seconds.

For an active/standby broker for high availability, Amazon MQ provides two ActiveMQ Web Console URLs, but only one URL is active at a time. Likewise, Amazon MQ provides two endpoints for each wire-level protocol, but only one endpoint is active in each pair at a time. The -1 and -2 suffixes denote a redundant pair. For wire-level protocol endpoints, you can allow your application to connect to either endpoint by using the Failover Transport.

The following diagram illustrates an active/standby broker for high availability.

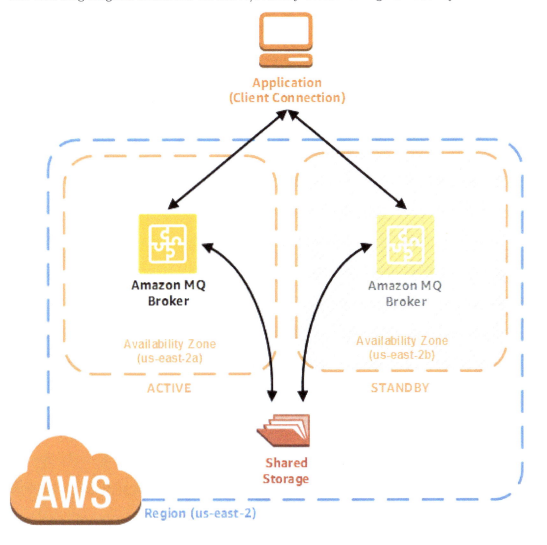

Amazon MQ Broker Configuration Lifecycle

Making changes to a configuration revision or an ActiveMQ user does *not* apply the changes immediately. To apply your changes, you must wait for the next 2-hour maintenance window or reboot the broker. For more information, see Amazon MQ Broker Configuration Lifecycle.

The following diagram illustrates the configuration lifecycle.

Important
The next scheduled 2-hour maintenance window triggers a reboot. If the broker is rebooted before the next scheduled maintenance window, the changes are applied after the reboot.

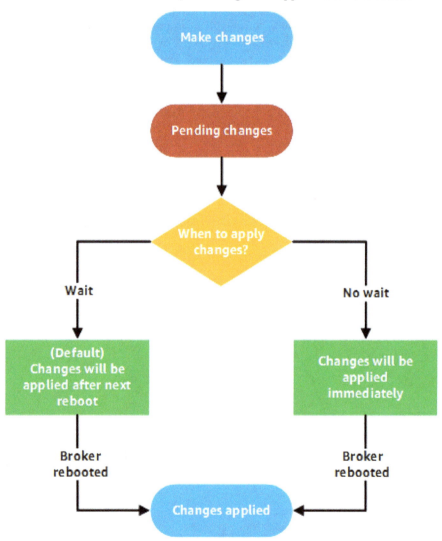

For information about creating, editing, and managing configurations, see the following:

- Tutorial: Creating and Applying Amazon MQ Broker Configurations
- Tutorial: Editing Amazon MQ Broker Configurations and Managing Configuration Revisions
- Amazon MQ Broker Configuration Parameters

For information about creating, editing, and deleting ActiveMQ users, see the following:

- Tutorial: Creating and Managing Amazon MQ Broker Users

- Users

Amazon MQ Broker Configuration Parameters

A *configuration* contains all of the settings for your ActiveMQ broker, in XML format (similar to ActiveMQ's `activemq.xml` file). You can create a configuration before creating any brokers. You can then apply the configuration to one or more brokers. For more information, see the following:

- Configuration

- Tutorial: Creating and Applying Amazon MQ Broker Configurations

- Tutorial: Editing Amazon MQ Broker Configurations and Managing Configuration Revisions

- Configurations

Working with Spring XML Configuration Files

ActiveMQ brokers are configured using Spring XML files. You can configure many aspects of your ActiveMQ broker, such as predefined destinations, destination policies, authorization policies, and plugins. Amazon MQ controls some of these configuration elements, such as network transports and storage. Other configuration options, such as creating networks of brokers, aren't currently supported.

The full set of supported configuration options is specified in the Amazon MQ XML schema. You can use this schema to validate and sanitize your configuration files. Amazon MQ also lets you provide configurations by uploading XML files. When you upload an XML file, Amazon MQ automatically sanitizes and removes invalid and prohibited configuration parameters according to the schema.

Note
You can use only static values for attributes. Amazon MQ sanitizes elements and attributes that contain Spring expressions, variables, and element references from your configuration.

- Working with Spring XML Configuration Files
- Elements Permitted in Amazon MQ Configurations
- Elements and Their Attributes Permitted in Amazon MQ Configurations
- Elements, Child Collection Elements, and Their Child Elements Permitted in Amazon MQ Configurations

Elements Permitted in Amazon MQ Configurations

The following is a detailed listing of the elements permitted in Amazon MQ configurations. For more information, see XML Configuration in the Apache ActiveMQ documentation.

Element
abortSlowAckConsumerStrategy (attributes)
abortSlowConsumerStrategy (attributes)
authorizationEntry (attributes)
authorizationMap (child collection elements)
authorizationPlugin (child collection elements)
broker (attributes
cachedMessageGroupMapFactory (attributes)
compositeQueue (attributes
compositeTopic (attributes
constantPendingMessageLimitStrategy (attributes)
discarding (attributes)
discardingDLQBrokerPlugin (attributes)
fileCursor
fileDurableSubscriberCursor
fileQueueCursor
filteredDestination (attributes)
fixedCountSubscriptionRecoveryPolicy (attributes)
fixedSizedSubscriptionRecoveryPolicy (attributes)
forcePersistencyModeBrokerPlugin (attributes)
individualDeadLetterStrategy (attributes)
lastImageSubscriptionRecoveryPolicy
messageGroupHashBucketFactory (attributes)
mirroredQueue (attributes)
noSubscriptionRecoveryPolicy
oldestMessageEvictionStrategy (attributes)
oldestMessageWithLowestPriorityEvictionStrategy (attributes)
policyEntry (attributes
policyMap (child collection elements)
prefetchRatePendingMessageLimitStrategy (attributes)
priorityDispatchPolicy
priorityNetworkDispatchPolicy
queryBasedSubscriptionRecoveryPolicy (attributes)
queue (attributes)
redeliveryPlugin (attributes
redeliveryPolicy (attributes)
redeliveryPolicyMap (child collection elements)
retainedMessageSubscriptionRecoveryPolicy (child collection elements)
roundRobinDispatchPolicy
sharedDeadLetterStrategy (attributes
simpleDispatchPolicy
simpleMessageGroupMapFactory
statisticsBrokerPlugin
storeCursor
storeDurableSubscriberCursor (attributes)
strictOrderDispatchPolicy
tempDestinationAuthorizationEntry (attributes)
tempQueue (attributes)
tempTopic (attributes)

Element
timedSubscriptionRecoveryPolicy (attributes)
timeStampingBrokerPlugin (attributes)
topic (attributes)
uniquePropertyMessageEvictionStrategy (attributes)
virtualDestinationInterceptor (child collection elements)
virtualTopic (attributes)
vmCursor
vmDurableCursor
vmQueueCursor

Elements and Their Attributes Permitted in Amazon MQ Configurations

The following is a detailed listing of the elements and their attributes permitted in Amazon MQ configurations. For more information, see XML Configuration in the Apache ActiveMQ documentation.

If you see an expand arrow () in the upper-right corner of the table, you can open the table in a new window. To close the window, choose the close button (**X**) in the lower-right corner.

[See the AWS documentation website for more details]

Elements, Child Collection Elements, and Their Child Elements Permitted in Amazon MQ Configurations

The following is a detailed listing of the elements, child collection elements, and their child elements permitted in Amazon MQ configurations. For more information, see XML Configuration in the Apache ActiveMQ documentation.

If you see an expand arrow () in the upper-right corner of the table, you can open the table in a new window. To close the window, choose the close button (**X**) in the lower-right corner.

[See the AWS documentation website for more details]

Amazon MQ Child Element Attributes

The following is a detailed explanation of child element attributes. For more information, see XML Configuration in the Apache ActiveMQ documentation.

authorizationEntry

authorizationEntry is a child of the `authorizationEntries` child collection element.

admin|read|write

Amazon MQ Default: Not configured.

Example Example Configuration

```
1  <authorizationPlugin>
2     <map>
3        <authorizationMap>
4           <authorizationEntries>
5              <authorizationEntry admin="admins,activemq-webconsole" read="admins,users,activemq-
                  webconsole" write="admins,activemq-webconsole" queue=">"/>
6              <authorizationEntry admin="admins,activemq-webconsole" read="admins,users,activemq-
                  webconsole" write="admins,activemq-webconsole" topic=">"/>
7           </authorizationEntries>
8        </authorizationMap>
9     </map>
10 </authorizationPlugin>
```

For more information, see Always Configure an Authorization Map.

kahaDB

kahaDB is a child of the `persistenceAdapter` child collection element.

concurrentStoreAndDispatchQueues

Amazon MQ Default: true

Example Example Configuration

```
1  <persistenceAdapter>
2     <kahaDB concurrentStoreAndDispatchQueues="false"/>
3  </persistenceAdapter>
```

For more information, see Disable Concurrent Store and Dispatch for Queues with Slow Consumers.

Working Examples of Using Java Message Service (JMS) with ActiveMQ

The following examples show how you can work with ActiveMQ programmatically:

- The OpenWire example Java code connects to a broker, creates a queue, and sends and receives a message. For a detailed breakdown and explanation, see Tutorial: Connecting a Java Application to Your Amazon MQ Broker.

- The MQTT example Java code connects to a broker, creates a topic, and publishes and receives a message.

- The STOMP+WSS example Java code connects to a broker, creates a queue, and publishes and receives a message.

Prerequisites

Enable Inbound Connections

1. Sign in to the Amazon MQ console.

2. From the broker list, choose the name of your broker (for example, **MyBroker**).

3. On the *MyBroker* page, in the **Connections** section, note the addresses and ports of the broker's ActiveMQ Web Console URL and wire-level protocols.

4. In the **Details** section, under **Security and network**, choose the name of your security group or ⬀.

   The **Security Groups** page of the EC2 Dashboard is displayed.

5. From the security group list, choose your security group.

6. At the bottom of the page, choose **Inbound**, and then choose **Edit**.

7. In the **Edit inbound rules** dialog box, add a rule for every URL or endpoint that you want to be publicly accessible (the following example shows how to do this for an ActiveMQ Web Console).

   1. Choose **Add Rule**.

   2. For **Type**, select **Custom TCP**.

   3. For **Port Range**, type the ActiveMQ Web Console port (`8162`).

   4. For **Source**, leave **Custom** selected and then type the IP address of the system that you want to be able to access the ActiveMQ Web Console (for example, `192.0.2.1`).

   5. Choose **Save**.

      Your broker can now accept inbound connections.

Add Java Dependencies

[OpenWire]

Add the `activemq-client.jar` and `activemq-pool.jar` packages to your Java class path. The following example shows these dependencies in a Maven project `pom.xml` file.

```
 1 <dependencies>
 2     <dependency>
 3         <groupId>org.apache.activemq</groupId>
 4         <artifactId>activemq-client</artifactId>
 5         <version>5.15.0</version>
 6     </dependency>
 7     <dependency>
 8         <groupId>org.apache.activemq</groupId>
 9         <artifactId>activemq-pool</artifactId>
10         <version>5.15.0</version>
11     </dependency>
12 </dependencies>
```

For more information about `activemq-client.jar`, see Initial Configuration in the Apache ActiveMQ documentation.

[MQTT]

Add the `org.eclipse.paho.client.mqttv3.jar` package to your Java class path. The following example shows this dependency in a Maven project `pom.xml` file.

```
 1 <dependencies>
 2     <dependency>
 3         <groupId>org.eclipse.paho</groupId>
 4         <artifactId>org.eclipse.paho.client.mqttv3</artifactId>
 5         <version>1.2.0</version>
 6     </dependency>
 7 </dependencies>
```

For more information about `org.eclipse.paho.client.mqttv3.jar`, see Eclipse Paho Java Client.

[STOMP+WSS]

Add the following packages to your Java class path:

- `spring-messaging.jar`

- `spring-websocket.jar`

- `javax.websocket-api.jar`

- `jetty-all.jar`

- `slf4j-simple.jar`

- `jackson-databind.jar`

The following example shows these dependencies in a Maven project `pom.xml` file.

```
 1 <dependencies>
 2     <dependency>
 3         <groupId>org.springframework</groupId>
 4         <artifactId>spring-messaging</artifactId>
 5         <version>5.0.5.RELEASE</version>
 6     </dependency>
 7     <dependency>
```

```
8        <groupId>org.springframework</groupId>
9        <artifactId>spring-websocket</artifactId>
10        <version>5.0.5.RELEASE</version>
11    </dependency>
12    <dependency>
13        <groupId>javax.websocket</groupId>
14        <artifactId>javax.websocket-api</artifactId>
15        <version>1.1</version>
16    </dependency>
17    <dependency>
18        <groupId>org.eclipse.jetty.aggregate</groupId>
19        <artifactId>jetty-all</artifactId>
20        <type>pom</type>
21        <version>9.3.3.v20150827</version>
22    </dependency>
23    <dependency>
24        <groupId>org.slf4j</groupId>
25        <artifactId>slf4j-simple</artifactId>
26        <version>1.6.6</version>
27    </dependency>
28    <dependency>
29        <groupId>com.fasterxml.jackson.core</groupId>
30        <artifactId>jackson-databind</artifactId>
31        <version>2.5.0</version>
32    </dependency>
33 </dependencies>
```

For more information, see STOMP Support in the Spring Framework documentation.

AmazonMQExample.java

[**OpenWire**]

```
1 /*
2  * Copyright 2010-2018 Amazon.com, Inc. or its affiliates. All Rights Reserved.
3  *
4  * Licensed under the Apache License, Version 2.0 (the "License").
5  * You may not use this file except in compliance with the License.
6  * A copy of the License is located at
7  *
8  *  https://aws.amazon.com/apache2.0
9  *
10  * or in the "license" file accompanying this file. This file is distributed
11  * on an "AS IS" BASIS, WITHOUT WARRANTIES OR CONDITIONS OF ANY KIND, either
12  * express or implied. See the License for the specific language governing
13  * permissions and limitations under the License.
14  *
15  */
16
17 import org.apache.activemq.ActiveMQConnectionFactory;
```

```java
18  import org.apache.activemq.jms.pool.PooledConnectionFactory;
19
20  import javax.jms.*;
21
22  public class AmazonMQExample {
23
24      // Specify the connection parameters.
25      private final static String WIRE_LEVEL_ENDPOINT
26              = "ssl://b-1234a5b6-78cd-901e-2fgh-3i45j6k17819-1.mq.us-east-2.amazonaws.com:61617";
27      private final static String ACTIVE_MQ_USERNAME = "MyUsername123";
28      private final static String ACTIVE_MQ_PASSWORD = "MyPassword456";
29
30      public static void main(String[] args) throws JMSException {
31          final ActiveMQConnectionFactory connectionFactory =
32                  createActiveMQConnectionFactory();
33          final PooledConnectionFactory pooledConnectionFactory =
34                  createPooledConnectionFactory(connectionFactory);
35
36          sendMessage(pooledConnectionFactory);
37          receiveMessage(connectionFactory);
38
39          pooledConnectionFactory.stop();
40      }
41
42      private static void
43      sendMessage(PooledConnectionFactory pooledConnectionFactory) throws JMSException {
44          // Establish a connection for the producer.
45          final Connection producerConnection = pooledConnectionFactory
46                  .createConnection();
47          producerConnection.start();
48
49          // Create a session.
50          final Session producerSession = producerConnection
51                  .createSession(false, Session.AUTO_ACKNOWLEDGE);
52
53          // Create a queue named "MyQueue".
54          final Destination producerDestination = producerSession
55                  .createQueue("MyQueue");
56
57          // Create a producer from the session to the queue.
58          final MessageProducer producer = producerSession
59                  .createProducer(producerDestination);
60          producer.setDeliveryMode(DeliveryMode.NON_PERSISTENT);
61
62          // Create a message.
63          final String text = "Hello from Amazon MQ!";
64          final TextMessage producerMessage = producerSession
65                  .createTextMessage(text);
66
67          // Send the message.
68          producer.send(producerMessage);
69          System.out.println("Message sent.");
70
71          // Clean up the producer.
```

```
72      producer.close();
73      producerSession.close();
74      producerConnection.close();
75  }
76
77  private static void
78  receiveMessage(ActiveMQConnectionFactory connectionFactory) throws JMSException {
79      // Establish a connection for the consumer.
80      // Note: Consumers should not use PooledConnectionFactory.
81      final Connection consumerConnection = connectionFactory.createConnection();
82      consumerConnection.start();
83
84      // Create a session.
85      final Session consumerSession = consumerConnection
86              .createSession(false, Session.AUTO_ACKNOWLEDGE);
87
88      // Create a queue named "MyQueue".
89      final Destination consumerDestination = consumerSession
90              .createQueue("MyQueue");
91
92      // Create a message consumer from the session to the queue.
93      final MessageConsumer consumer = consumerSession
94              .createConsumer(consumerDestination);
95
96      // Begin to wait for messages.
97      final Message consumerMessage = consumer.receive(1000);
98
99      // Receive the message when it arrives.
100     final TextMessage consumerTextMessage = (TextMessage) consumerMessage;
101     System.out.println("Message received: " + consumerTextMessage.getText());
102
103     // Clean up the consumer.
104     consumer.close();
105     consumerSession.close();
106     consumerConnection.close();
107 }
108
109 private static PooledConnectionFactory
110 createPooledConnectionFactory(ActiveMQConnectionFactory connectionFactory) {
111     // Create a pooled connection factory.
112     final PooledConnectionFactory pooledConnectionFactory =
113             new PooledConnectionFactory();
114     pooledConnectionFactory.setConnectionFactory(connectionFactory);
115     pooledConnectionFactory.setMaxConnections(10);
116     return pooledConnectionFactory;
117 }
118
119 private static ActiveMQConnectionFactory createActiveMQConnectionFactory() {
120     // Create a connection factory.
121     final ActiveMQConnectionFactory connectionFactory =
122             new ActiveMQConnectionFactory(WIRE_LEVEL_ENDPOINT);
123
124     // Pass the username and password.
125     connectionFactory.setUserName(ACTIVE_MQ_USERNAME);
```

```
126        connectionFactory.setPassword(ACTIVE_MQ_PASSWORD);
127        return connectionFactory;
128    }
129 }
```

[MQTT]

```
1  /*
2   * Copyright 2010-2018 Amazon.com, Inc. or its affiliates. All Rights Reserved.
3   *
4   * Licensed under the Apache License, Version 2.0 (the "License").
5   * You may not use this file except in compliance with the License.
6   * A copy of the License is located at
7   *
8   *  https://aws.amazon.com/apache2.0
9   *
10  * or in the "license" file accompanying this file. This file is distributed
11  * on an "AS IS" BASIS, WITHOUT WARRANTIES OR CONDITIONS OF ANY KIND, either
12  * express or implied. See the License for the specific language governing
13  * permissions and limitations under the License.
14  *
15  */
16
17 import org.eclipse.paho.client.mqttv3.*;
18
19 public class AmazonMQExampleMqtt implements MqttCallback {
20
21     // Specify the connection parameters.
22     private final static String WIRE_LEVEL_ENDPOINT =
23             "ssl://b-1234a5b6-78cd-901e-2fgh-3i45j6k17819-1.mq.us-east-2.amazonaws.com:8883";
24     private final static String ACTIVE_MQ_USERNAME = "MyUsername123";
25     private final static String ACTIVE_MQ_PASSWORD = "MyPassword456";
26
27     public static void main(String[] args) throws Exception {
28         new AmazonMQExampleMqtt().run();
29     }
30
31     private void run() throws MqttException, InterruptedException {
32
33         // Specify the topic name and the message text.
34         final String topic = "myTopic";
35         final String text = "Hello from Amazon MQ!";
36
37         // Create the MQTT client and specify the connection options.
38         final String clientId = "abc123";
39         final MqttClient client = new MqttClient(WIRE_LEVEL_ENDPOINT, clientId);
40         final MqttConnectOptions connOpts = new MqttConnectOptions();
41
42         // Pass the username and password.
43         connOpts.setUserName(ACTIVE_MQ_USERNAME);
44         connOpts.setPassword(ACTIVE_MQ_PASSWORD.toCharArray());
45
46         // Create a session and subscribe to a topic filter.
```

63

```
47        client.connect(connOpts);
48        client.setCallback(this);
49        client.subscribe("+");
50
51        // Create a message.
52        final MqttMessage message = new MqttMessage(text.getBytes());
53
54        // Publish the message to a topic.
55        client.publish(topic, message);
56        System.out.println("Published message.");
57
58        // Wait for the message to be received.
59        Thread.sleep(3000L);
60
61        // Clean up the connection.
62        client.disconnect();
63    }
64
65    @Override
66    public void connectionLost(Throwable cause) {
67        System.out.println("Lost connection.");
68    }
69
70    @Override
71    public void messageArrived(String topic, MqttMessage message) throws MqttException {
72        System.out.println("Received message from topic " + topic + ": " + message);
73    }
74
75    @Override
76    public void deliveryComplete(IMqttDeliveryToken token) {
77        System.out.println("Delivered message.");
78    }
79 }
```

[STOMP+WSS]

```
1  /*
2   * Copyright 2010-2018 Amazon.com, Inc. or its affiliates. All Rights Reserved.
3   *
4   * Licensed under the Apache License, Version 2.0 (the "License").
5   * You may not use this file except in compliance with the License.
6   * A copy of the License is located at
7   *
8   *  https://aws.amazon.com/apache2.0
9   *
10  * or in the "license" file accompanying this file. This file is distributed
11  * on an "AS IS" BASIS, WITHOUT WARRANTIES OR CONDITIONS OF ANY KIND, either
12  * express or implied. See the License for the specific language governing
13  * permissions and limitations under the License.
14  *
15  */
16
17 import org.springframework.messaging.converter.StringMessageConverter;
```

```
18 import org.springframework.messaging.simp.stomp.*;
19 import org.springframework.web.socket.WebSocketHttpHeaders;
20 import org.springframework.web.socket.client.WebSocketClient;
21 import org.springframework.web.socket.client.standard.StandardWebSocketClient;
22 import org.springframework.web.socket.messaging.WebSocketStompClient;
23
24 import java.lang.reflect.Type;
25
26 public class AmazonMQExampleStompWss {
27
28     // Specify the connection parameters.
29     private final static String DESTINATION = "/queue";
30     private final static String WIRE_LEVEL_ENDPOINT =
31             "wss://b-1234a5b6-78cd-901e-2fgh-3i45j6k17819-1.mq.us-east-2.amazonaws.com:61619";
32     private final static String ACTIVE_MQ_USERNAME = "MyUsername123";
33     private final static String ACTIVE_MQ_PASSWORD = "MyPassword456";
34
35     public static void main(String[] args) throws Exception {
36         final AmazonMQExampleStompWss example = new AmazonMQExampleStompWss();
37
38         final StompSession stompSession = example.connect();
39         System.out.println("Subscribed to a destination using session.");
40         example.subscribeToDestination(stompSession);
41
42         System.out.println("Sent message to session.");
43         example.sendMessage(stompSession);
44         Thread.sleep(60000);
45     }
46
47     private StompSession connect() throws Exception {
48         // Create a client.
49         final WebSocketClient client = new StandardWebSocketClient();
50         final WebSocketStompClient stompClient = new WebSocketStompClient(client);
51         stompClient.setMessageConverter(new StringMessageConverter());
52
53         final WebSocketHttpHeaders headers = new WebSocketHttpHeaders();
54
55         // Create headers with authentication parameters.
56         final StompHeaders head = new StompHeaders();
57         head.add(StompHeaders.LOGIN, ACTIVE_MQ_USERNAME);
58         head.add(StompHeaders.PASSCODE, ACTIVE_MQ_PASSWORD);
59
60         final StompSessionHandler sessionHandler = new MySessionHandler();
61
62         // Create a connection.
63         return stompClient.connect(WIRE_LEVEL_ENDPOINT, headers, head,
64                 sessionHandler).get();
65     }
66
67     private void subscribeToDestination(final StompSession stompSession) {
68         stompSession.subscribe(DESTINATION, new MyFrameHandler());
69     }
70
71     private void sendMessage(final StompSession stompSession) {
```

```
72          stompSession.send(DESTINATION, "Hello from Amazon MQ!".getBytes());
73      }
74
75      private static class MySessionHandler extends StompSessionHandlerAdapter {
76          public void afterConnected(final StompSession stompSession,
77                                      final StompHeaders stompHeaders) {
78              System.out.println("Connected to broker.");
79          }
80      }
81
82      private static class MyFrameHandler implements StompFrameHandler {
83          public Type getPayloadType(final StompHeaders headers) {
84              return String.class;
85          }
86
87          public void handleFrame(final StompHeaders stompHeaders,
88                                   final Object message) {
89              System.out.print("Received message from topic: " + message);
90          }
91      }
92 }
```

Migrating to Amazon MQ

Use the following topics to get started with migrating your on-premises message broker to Amazon MQ.

- Migrating to Amazon MQ without Service Interruption
- Migrating to Amazon MQ with Service Interruption

Migrating to Amazon MQ without Service Interruption

The following diagrams illustrate the scenario of migrating from an on-premises message broker to an Amazon MQ broker in the AWS Cloud without service interruption.

Important
This scenario might cause messages to be delivered out of order. If you're concerned about message ordering, follow the steps in Migrating to Amazon MQ with Service Interruption.

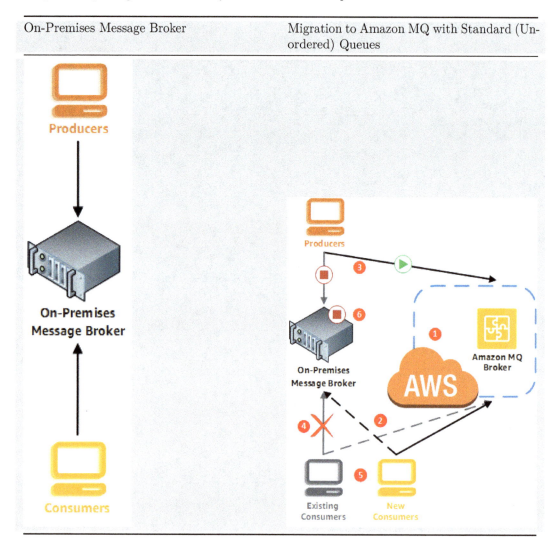

On-Premises Message Broker	Migration to Amazon MQ with Standard (Un-ordered) Queues

To migrate to Amazon MQ without service interruption

1 Create and configure an Amazon MQ broker and note your broker's endpoint, for example:

```
1 ssl://b-1234a5b6-78cd-901e-2fgh-3i45j6k17819-1.mq.us-east-2.amazonaws.com:61617
```

2 For either of the following cases, use the Failover Transport to allow your consumers to randomly connect to your on-premises broker's endpoint or your Amazon MQ broker's endpoint. For example:

```
1 failover:(ssl://on-premises-broker.example.com:61617,ssl://b-1234a5b6-78cd-901e-2fgh-3
    i45j6k17819-1.mq.us-east-2.amazonaws.com:61617)?randomize=true
```

Do one of the following:

- One by one, point each existing consumer to your Amazon MQ broker's endpoint.

- Create new consumers and point them to your Amazon MQ broker's endpoint. **Note**
  If you scale up your consumer fleet during the migration process, it is a best practice to scale it down afterward.

3 One by one, stop each existing producer, point the producer to your Amazon MQ broker's endpoint, and then restart the producer.

4 Wait for your consumers to drain the destinations on your on-premises broker.

5 Change your consumers' Failover transport to include only your Amazon MQ broker's endpoint. For example:

```
1 failover:(ssl://b-1234a5b6-78cd-901e-2fgh-3i45j6k17819-1.mq.us-east-2.amazonaws.com:61617)
```

6 Stop your on-premises broker.

Migrating to Amazon MQ with Service Interruption

The following diagrams illustrate the scenario of migrating from an on-premises message broker to an Amazon MQ broker in the AWS Cloud with service interruption.

Important

This scenario requires you to point your producer to your Amazon MQ broker's endpoint *before* you do the same for your consumers. This sequence ensures that any messages in a FIFO (first-in-first-out) queue maintain their order during the migration process. If you're not concerned about message ordering, follow the steps in Migrating to Amazon MQ without Service Interruption.

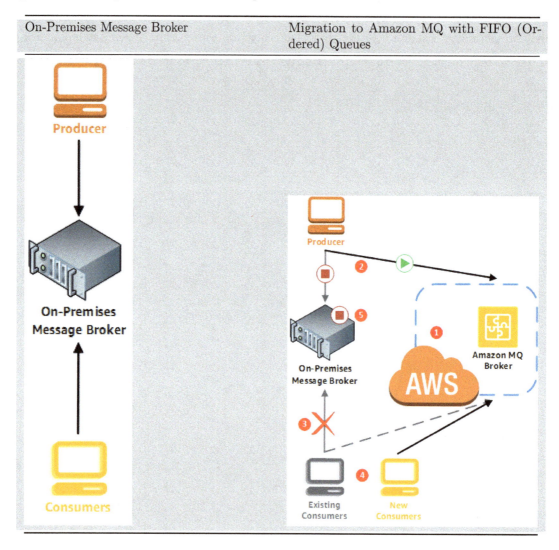

To migrate to Amazon MQ with service interruption

1 Create and configure an Amazon MQ broker and note your broker's endpoint, for example:

```
1 ssl://b-1234a5b6-78cd-901e-2fgh-3i45j6k17819-1.mq.us-east-2.amazonaws.com:61617
```

2 Stop your existing producer, point the producer to your Amazon MQ broker's endpoint, and then restart the producer.

Important

This step requires an interruption of your application's functionality because no consumers are yet consuming messages from the Amazon MQ broker.

3 Wait for your consumers to drain the destinations on your on-premises broker.

4 Do one of the following:

- One by one, point each existing consumer to your Amazon MQ broker's endpoint.

- Create new consumers and point them to your Amazon MQ broker's endpoint. **Note**
  If you scale up your consumer fleet during the migration process, it is a best practice to scale it down afterward.

5 Stop your on-premises broker.

Best Practices for Amazon MQ

Use these best practices to make the most of Amazon MQ.

- Using Amazon MQ Securely
- Connecting to Amazon MQ
- Ensuring Effective Amazon MQ Performance

Using Amazon MQ Securely

The following design patterns can improve the security of your Amazon MQ broker.

- Prefer Brokers without Public Accessibility
- Always Use Client-Side Encryption as a Complement to TLS
- Always Configure an Authorization Map
- Always Configure a System Group

Prefer Brokers without Public Accessibility

Brokers created without public accessibility can't be accessed from outside of your VPC. This greatly reduces your broker's susceptibility to Distributed Denial of Service (DDoS) attacks from the public Internet. For more information, see How to Help Prepare for DDoS Attacks by Reducing Your Attack Surface on the AWS Security Blog.

Always Use Client-Side Encryption as a Complement to TLS

You can access your brokers using the following protocols with TLS enabled:

- AMQP

- MQTT

- MQTT over WebSocket

- OpenWire

- STOMP

- STOMP over WebSocket

Amazon MQ encrypts messages at rest and in transit using encryption keys that it manages and stores securely. For additional security, we highly recommend designing your application to use client-side encryption. For more information, see the *AWS Encryption SDK Developer Guide*.

Always Configure an Authorization Map

Because ActiveMQ has no authorization map configured by default, any authenticated user can perform any action on the broker. Thus, it is a best practice to restrict permissions *by group*.

Always Configure a System Group

Amazon MQ uses a *system group* (called `activemq-webconsole`) to allow the ActiveMQ Web Console to communicate with the ActiveMQ broker.

The settings for the `activemq-webconsole` group in the authorization map restrict which operations can be performed on queues or topics from the web console. For more information and an example configuration, see authorizationEntry.

Important
If you specify an authorization map which doesn't include the `activemq-webconsole` group, you won't be able to use the ActiveMQ Web Console because the group isn't authorized to send messages to, or receive messages from, the Amazon MQ broker.

Connecting to Amazon MQ

The following design patterns can improve the effectiveness of your application's connection to your Amazon MQ broker.

- Never Modify or Delete the Amazon MQ Elastic Network Interface
- Always Use Connection Pooling
- Always Use the Failover Transport to Connect to Multiple Broker Endpoints
- Avoid Using Message Selectors
- Prefer Virtual Destinations to Durable Subscriptions

Never Modify or Delete the Amazon MQ Elastic Network Interface

When you first create an Amazon MQ broker, Amazon MQ provisions an elastic network interface in the Virtual Private Cloud (VPC) under your account and, thus, requires a number of EC2 permissions. The network interface allows your client (producer or consumer) to communicate with the Amazon MQ broker. The network interface is considered to be within the *service scope* of Amazon MQ, despite being part of your account's VPC.

Warning
You must not modify or delete this network interface. Modifying or deleting the network interface can cause a permanent loss of connection between your VPC and your broker.
Currently, you can't recover your broker if you delete its network interface. You can only recreate your broker.

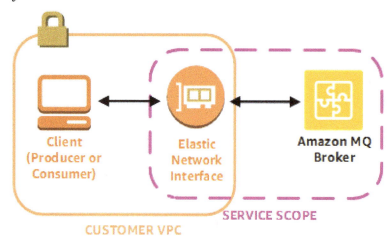

Always Use Connection Pooling

In a scenario with a single producer and single consumer (such as the Getting Started with Amazon MQ tutorial), you can use a single http://activemq.apache.org/maven/apidocs/org/apache/activemq/ActiveMQConnectionFactory.html class for every producer and consumer. For example:

```
1 // Create a connection factory.
2 final ActiveMQConnectionFactory connectionFactory = new ActiveMQConnectionFactory(
      wireLevelEndpoint);
3
4 // Pass the username and password.
5 connectionFactory.setUserName(activeMqUsername);
6 connectionFactory.setPassword(activeMqPassword);
7
```

```
8  // Establish a connection for the consumer.
9  final Connection consumerConnection = connectionFactory.createConnection();
10 consumerConnection.start();
```

However, in more realistic scenarios with multiple producers and consumers, it can be costly and inefficient to create a large number of connections for multiple producers. In these scenarios, you should group multiple producer requests using the http://activemq.apache.org/maven/apidocs/org/apache/activemq/jms/pool/PooledConnectionFactory.html class. For example:

Note
Message consumers should *never* use the `PooledConnectionFactory` class.

```
1  // Create a connection factory.
2  final ActiveMQConnectionFactory connectionFactory = new ActiveMQConnectionFactory(
       wireLevelEndpoint);
3
4  // Pass the username and password.
5  connectionFactory.setUserName(activeMqUsername);
6  connectionFactory.setPassword(activeMqPassword);
7
8  // Create a pooled connection factory.
9  final PooledConnectionFactory pooledConnectionFactory = new PooledConnectionFactory();
10 pooledConnectionFactory.setConnectionFactory(connectionFactory);
11 pooledConnectionFactory.setMaxConnections(10);
12
13 // Establish a connection for the producer.
14 final Connection producerConnection = pooledConnectionFactory.createConnection();
15 producerConnection.start();
```

Always Use the Failover Transport to Connect to Multiple Broker Endpoints

If you need your application to connect to multiple broker endpoints—for example, when you use an active/standby broker for high availability or when you migrate from an on-premises message broker to Amazon MQ—use the Failover Transport to allow your consumers to randomly connect to either one. For example:

```
1  failover:(ssl://b-1234a5b6-78cd-901e-2fgh-3i45j6k17819-1.mq.us-east-2.amazonaws.com:61617,ssl://
       b-987615k4-32ji-109h-8gfe-7d65c4b132a1-2.mq.us-east-2.amazonaws.com:61617)?randomize=true
```

Avoid Using Message Selectors

It is possible to use JMS selectors to attach filters to topic subscriptions (to route messages to consumers based on their content). However, the use of JMS selectors fills up the Amazon MQ broker's filter buffer, preventing it from filtering messages.

In general, avoid letting consumers route messages because, for optimal decoupling of consumers and producers, both the consumer and the producer should be ephemeral.

Prefer Virtual Destinations to Durable Subscriptions

A durable subscription can help ensure that the consumer receives all messages published to a topic, for example, after a lost connection is restored. However, the use of durable subscriptions also precludes the use of competing consumers and might have performance issues at scale. Consider using virtual destinations instead.

Ensuring Effective Amazon MQ Performance

The following design patterns can improve the effectiveness and performance of your Amazon MQ broker.

Disable Concurrent Store and Dispatch for Queues with Slow Consumers

By default, Amazon MQ optimizes for queues with fast consumers:

- Consumers are considered to be *fast* if they are able to keep up with the rate of messages generated by producers.

- Consumers are considered to be *slow* if a queue builds a backlog of unacknowledged messages, potentially causing a decrease in producer throughput.

To instruct Amazon MQ to optimize for queues with slow consumers, set the `concurrentStoreAndDispatchQueues` attribute to `false`. For an example configuration, see `concurrentStoreAndDispatchQueues`.

Limits in Amazon MQ

This topic lists limits within Amazon MQ. Many of the following limits can be changed for specific AWS accounts. To request an increase for a limit, see AWS Service Limits in the *Amazon Web Services General Reference.*

- Limits Related to Brokers
- Limits Related to Configurations
- Limits Related to Users
- Limits Related to Data Storage
- Limits Related to API Throttling

Brokers

The following table lists limits related to Amazon MQ brokers.

Limit	Description
Broker name	[See the AWS documentation website for more details]
Brokers per broker instance type, per AWS account, per region	20
Broker configuration history depth	10
Security groups per broker	5
Destinations (queues and topics) monitored in CloudWatch	CloudWatch monitors only the first 200 destinations.

Configurations

The following table lists limits related to Amazon MQ configurations.

Limit	Description
Configuration name	[See the AWS documentation website for more details]
Configurations per AWS account	1,000
Revisions per configuration	300

Users

The following table lists limits related to Amazon MQ users.

Limit	Description
Username	[See the AWS documentation website for more details]
Password	[See the AWS documentation website for more details]
Users per broker	250
Groups per user	5

Data Storage

The following table lists limits related to Amazon MQ data storage.

Limit	Description
Storage capacity per broker	200 GB
Data store	Amazon MQ uses Apache KahaDB as its data store. Other data stores, such as JDBC and LevelDB, aren't supported.

API Throttling

The following throttling limits are aggregated per AWS account, *across all Amazon MQ APIs* to maintain service bandwidth.

Note
These limits don't apply to ActiveMQ messaging APIs.

Bucket Size	Refill Rate per Second
100	15

Monitoring Amazon MQ using Amazon CloudWatch

Amazon MQ and Amazon CloudWatch are integrated so you can use CloudWatch to view and analyze metrics for your ActiveMQ broker and the broker's destinations (queues and topics). You can view and analyze your Amazon MQ metrics from the CloudWatch console, the AWS CLI, or the CloudWatch CLI. CloudWatch metrics for Amazon MQ are automatically polled from the broker and then pushed to CloudWatch every minute.

For information about accessing Amazon MQ CloudWatch metrics, see Tutorial: Accessing CloudWatch Metrics for Amazon MQ.

Note
The following statistics are valid for all of the metrics:
`Average Minimum Maximum Sum`

The `AWS/AmazonMQ` namespace includes the following metrics.

Broker Metrics

Metric	Unit	Description
CpuUtilization	Percent	The percentage of allocated EC2 compute units that the broker currently uses.
HeapUsage	Percent	The percentage of the ActiveMQ JVM memory limit that the broker currently uses.
NetworkIn	Bytes	The volume of incoming traffic for the broker.
NetworkOut	Bytes	The volume of outgoing traffic for the broker.
TotalMessageCount	Count	The number of messages stored on the broker.

Dimension for Broker Metrics

Dimension	Description
Broker	The name of the broker. A single-instance broker has the suffix -1. An active-standby broker for high availability has the suffixes -1 and -2 for its redundant pair.

Destination (Queue and Topic) Metrics

Important
The following metrics record only values since CloudWatch polled the metrics last:
`EnqueueCount ExpiredCount DequeueCount DispatchCount`

Metric	Unit	Description
ConsumerCount	Count	The number of consumers subscribed to the destination.

Metric	Unit	Description
EnqueueCount	Count	The number of messages sent to the destination.
EnqueueTime	Time (milliseconds)	The amount of time it takes the broker to accept a message from the producer and send it to the destination.
ExpiredCount	Count	The number of messages that couldn't be delivered because they expired.
DispatchCount	Count	The number of messages sent to consumers.
DequeueCount	Count	The number of messages acknowledged by consumers.
MemoryUsage	Percent	The percentage of the memory limit that the destination currently uses.
ProducerCount	Count	The number of producers for the destination.
QueueSize	Count	The number of messages in the queue. This metric applies only to queues.

Dimensions for Destination (Queue and Topic) Metrics

Dimension	Description
Broker	The name of the broker. A single-instance broker has the suffix -1. An active-standby broker for high availability has the suffixes -1 and -2 for its redundant pair.
Topic or Queue	The name of the topic or queue.

Amazon MQ Security

This section provides information about Amazon MQ and ActiveMQ authentication and authorization. For information about security best practices, see Using Amazon MQ Securely.

- API Authentication and Authorization for Amazon MQ
- Messaging Authentication and Authorization for ActiveMQ

API Authentication and Authorization for Amazon MQ

Amazon MQ uses standard AWS request signing for API authentication. For more information, see Signing AWS API Requests in the *AWS General Reference*.

Note
Currently, Amazon MQ doesn't support IAM authentication using resource-based permissions or resource-based policies.

To authorize AWS users to work with brokers, configurations, and users, you must edit your IAM policy permissions.

- IAM Permissions Required to Create an Amazon MQ Broker
- Amazon MQ REST API Permissions Reference

IAM Permissions Required to Create an Amazon MQ Broker

To create a broker, you must either use the `AmazonMQFullAccess` IAM policy or include the following EC2 permissions in your IAM policy.

The following custom policy is comprised of two statements (one conditional) which grant permissions to manipulate the resources which Amazon MQ requires to create an ActiveMQ broker.

Important
The `ec2:CreateNetworkInterface` action is required to allow Amazon MQ to create an elastic network interface (ENI) in your account on your behalf. The `ec2:CreateNetworkInterfacePermission` action authorizes Amazon MQ to attach the ENI to an ActiveMQ broker. The `ec2:AuthorizedService` condition key ensures that ENI permissions can be granted only to Amazon MQ service accounts.

```
1  {
2      "Version": "2012-10-17",
3      "Statement": [{
4          "Action": [
5              "mq:*",
6              "[ec2:CreateNetworkInterface](http://docs.aws.amazon.com/AWSEC2/latest/APIReference/
                  API_CreateNetworkInterface.html)",
7              "[ec2:DeleteNetworkInterface](http://docs.aws.amazon.com/AWSEC2/latest/APIReference/
                  API_DeleteNetworkInterface.html)",
8              "[ec2:DetachNetworkInterface](http://docs.aws.amazon.com/AWSEC2/latest/APIReference/
                  API_DetachNetworkInterface.html)",
9              "[ec2:DescribeInternetGateways](http://docs.aws.amazon.com/AWSEC2/latest/
                  APIReference/API_DescribeInternetGateways.html)",
10             "[ec2:DescribeNetworkInterfaces](http://docs.aws.amazon.com/AWSEC2/latest/
                  APIReference/API_DescribeNetworkInterfaces.html)",
11             "[ec2:DescribeRouteTables](http://docs.aws.amazon.com/AWSEC2/latest/APIReference/
                  API_DescribeRouteTables.html)",
12             "[ec2:DescribeSecurityGroups](http://docs.aws.amazon.com/AWSEC2/latest/APIReference/
                  API_DescribeSecurityGroups.html)",
13             "[ec2:DescribeSubnets](http://docs.aws.amazon.com/AWSEC2/latest/APIReference/
                  API_DescribeSubnets.html)",
14             "[ec2:DescribeVpcs](http://docs.aws.amazon.com/AWSEC2/latest/APIReference/
                  API_DescribeVpcs.html)"
15         ],
16         "Effect": "Allow",
17         "Resource": "*"
18     },{
```

```
19      "Action": [
20          "[ec2:CreateNetworkInterfacePermission](http://docs.aws.amazon.com/AWSEC2/latest/
                APIReference/API_CreateNetworkInterfacePermission.html)",
21          "[ec2:DeleteNetworkInterfacePermission](http://docs.aws.amazon.com/AWSEC2/latest/
                APIReference/API_DeleteNetworkInterfacePermission.html)",
22          "[ec2:DescribeNetworkInterfacePermission](http://docs.aws.amazon.com/AWSEC2/latest/
                APIReference/API_DescribeNetworkInterfacePermissions.html)"
23      ],
24      "Effect": "Allow",
25      "Resource": "*",
26      "Condition": {
27          "StringEquals": {
28              "[ec2:AuthorizedService](http://docs.aws.amazon.com/IAM/latest/UserGuide/
                    list_amazonec2.html#amazonec2-ec2_AuthorizedService)": "mq.amazonaws.com"
29          }
30      }
31  }]
32 }
```

For more information, see Step 2: Create an IAM User and Get Your AWS Credentials and Never Modify or Delete the Amazon MQ Elastic Network Interface.

Amazon MQ REST API Permissions Reference

The following table lists Amazon MQ REST APIs and the corresponding IAM permissions.

Amazon MQ REST APIs and Required Permissions

Amazon MQ REST APIs	Required Permissions
http://docs.aws.amazon.com/amazon-mq/latest/api-reference/rest-api-brokers.html#rest-api-brokers-methods-post	mq:CreateBroker
http://docs.aws.amazon.com/amazon-mq/latest/api-reference/rest-api-configurations.html#rest-api-configurations-methods-post	mq:CreateConfiguration
http://docs.aws.amazon.com/amazon-mq/latest/api-reference/rest-api-user.html#rest-api-user-methods-post	mq:CreateUser
http://docs.aws.amazon.com/amazon-mq/latest/api-reference/rest-api-broker.html#rest-api-broker-methods-delete	mq:DeleteBroker
http://docs.aws.amazon.com/amazon-mq/latest/api-reference/rest-api-user.html#rest-api-user-methods-delete	mq:DeleteUser
http://docs.aws.amazon.com/amazon-mq/latest/api-reference/rest-api-broker.html#rest-api-broker-methods-get	mq:DescribeBroker
http://docs.aws.amazon.com/amazon-mq/latest/api-reference/rest-api-configuration.html#rest-api-configuration-methods-get	mq:DescribeConfiguration

Amazon MQ REST APIs	Required Permissions
http://docs.aws.amazon.com/amazon-mq/latest/api-reference/rest-api-configuration-revision.html#rest-api-configuration-revision-methods-get	mq:DescribeConfigurationRevision
http://docs.aws.amazon.com/amazon-mq/latest/api-reference/rest-api-user.html#rest-api-user-methods-get	mq:DescribeUser
http://docs.aws.amazon.com/amazon-mq/latest/api-reference/rest-api-brokers.html#rest-api-brokers-methods-get	mq:ListBrokers
http://docs.aws.amazon.com/amazon-mq/latest/api-reference/rest-api-configuration-revisions.html#rest-api-configuration-revisions-methods-get	mq:ListConfigurationRevisions
http://docs.aws.amazon.com/amazon-mq/latest/api-reference/rest-api-configurations.html#rest-api-configurations-methods-get	mq:ListConfigurations
http://docs.aws.amazon.com/amazon-mq/latest/api-reference/rest-api-users.html#rest-api-users-methods-get	mq:ListUsers
http://docs.aws.amazon.com/amazon-mq/latest/api-reference/rest-api-broker-reboot.html#rest-api-broker-reboot-methods-post	mq:RebootBroker
http://docs.aws.amazon.com/amazon-mq/latest/api-reference/rest-api-broker.html#rest-api-broker-methods-put	mq:UpdateBroker
http://docs.aws.amazon.com/amazon-mq/latest/api-reference/rest-api-configuration.html#rest-api-configuration-methods-put	mq:UpdateConfiguration
http://docs.aws.amazon.com/amazon-mq/latest/api-reference/rest-api-user.html#rest-api-user-methods-put	mq:UpdateUser

Messaging Authentication and Authorization for ActiveMQ

You can access your brokers using the following protocols with TLS enabled:

- AMQP

- MQTT

- MQTT over WebSocket

- OpenWire

- STOMP

- STOMP over WebSocket

Amazon MQ uses native ActiveMQ authentication. For information about restrictions related to ActiveMQ usernames and passwords, see Users.

To authorize ActiveMQ users and groups to works with queues and topics, you must edit your broker's configuration. For information about configuring Amazon MQ, see Amazon MQ Broker Configuration Parameters.

Note

Currently, Amazon MQ doesn't support Client Certificate Authentication or plugins for Java Authentication and Authorization Service (JAAS).

Related Resources

Amazon MQ Resources

The following table lists useful resources for working with Amazon MQ.

Resource	Description
Amazon MQ REST API Reference	Descriptions of REST resources, example requests, HTTP methods, schemas, parameters, and the errors that the service returns.
Amazon MQ in the *AWS CLI Command Reference*	Descriptions of the AWS CLI commands that you can use to work with message brokers.
Regions and Endpoints	Information about Amazon MQ regions and endpoints
Product Page	The primary web page for information about Amazon MQ.
Discussion Forum	A community-based forum for developers to discuss technical questions related to Amazon MQ.
AWS Premium Support Information	The primary web page for information about AWS Premium Support, a one-on-one, fast-response support channel to help you build and run applications on AWS infrastructure services

Apache ActiveMQ Resources

The following table lists useful resources for working with Apache ActiveMQ.

Resource	Description
Apache ActiveMQ Getting Started Guide	The official documentation of Apache ActiveMQ.
ActiveMQ in Action	A guide to Apache ActiveMQ that covers the anatomy of JMS messages, connectors, message persistence, authentication, and authorization.
Cross-Language Clients	A list of programming languages and corresponding Apache ActiveMQ libraries. See also ActiveMQ Client and QpidJMS Client.

Amazon MQ Release Notes

The following table lists Amazon MQ feature releases and improvements. For changes to the *Amazon MQ Developer Guide*, see Amazon MQ Document History.

Date	Feature Release
June 7, 2018	The Amazon MQ console supports German, Brazilian Portuguese, Spanish, Italian, and Traditional Chinese.
May 17, 2018	The limit of number of users per broker is 250. For more information, see Users.
March 13, 2018	Creating a broker takes about 15 minutes. For more information, see Finish creating the broker.
March 1, 2018	You can configure the concurrent store and dispatch for Apache KahaDB using the `concurrentStoreAndDispatchQueues` attribute.
January 10, 2018	The following changes affect the Amazon MQ console: [See the AWS documentation website for more details]
January 9, 2018	[See the AWS documentation website for more details]
November 28, 2017	This is the initial release of Amazon MQ and the Amazon MQ Developer Guide.[See the AWS documentation website for more details]

Amazon MQ Document History

The following table lists changes to the *Amazon MQ Developer Guide*. For Amazon MQ feature releases and improvements, see Amazon MQ Release Notes.

Date	Documentation Update
June 4, 2018	In addition to GitHub, HTML, PDF, and Kindle, the *Amazon MQ Developer Guide* release notes are available as an RSS feed.
May 29, 2018	[See the AWS documentation website for more details]
May 24, 2018	Corrected the wire-level endpoint port in the MQTT Java example in the Working Examples of Using Java Message Service (JMS) with ActiveMQ section.
May 22, 2018	Corrected the information in all Java dependency sections.
May 17, 2018	Corrected the information in the Users section.
May 15, 2018	Corrected the information in the Ensuring Effective Amazon MQ Performance section.
May 8, 2018	[See the AWS documentation website for more details]
May 7, 2018	[See the AWS documentation website for more details]
May 1, 2018	Clarified the information about the maintenance window for active/standby brokers for high availability in the following sections: [See the AWS documentation website for more details]
April 27, 2018	Rewrote the following sections and optimized example Java code to match the recommendation to use connection pooling only for producers, not consumers: [See the AWS documentation website for more details]
April 26, 2018	Added an MQTT Java example to the Working Examples of Using Java Message Service (JMS) with ActiveMQ section. The MQTT example Java code connects to a broker, creates a topic, and publishes and receives a message.
April 6, 2018	Updated the Frequently Viewed Amazon MQ Topics section.
April 4, 2018	Renamed the Communicating with Amazon MQ section to Connecting to Amazon MQ.
April 3, 2018	Clarified and corrected the information in the the Disable Concurrent Store and Dispatch for Queues with Slow Consumers section.

Date	Documentation Update
April 2, 2018	Moved the Concurrent Store and Dispatch for Queues in Amazon MQ section to the Disable Concurrent Store and Dispatch for Queues with Slow Consumers section.
March 27, 2018	[See the AWS documentation website for more details]
March 22, 2018	Clarified the following statement throughout this guide: Amazon MQ encrypts messages at rest and in transit using encryption keys that it manages and stores securely. For additional security, we highly recommend designing your application to use client-side encryption. For more information, see the AWS Encryption SDK Developer Guide.
March 19, 2018	Clarified the following statement throughout this guide: An Active/standby broker for high availability is comprised of two brokers in two different Availability Zones, configured in a redundant pair. These brokers communicate synchronously with your application, and with a shared storage location.
March 15, 2018	[See the AWS documentation website for more details]
March 12, 2018	[See the AWS documentation website for more details]
March 9, 2018	[See the AWS documentation website for more details]
March 8, 2018	[See the AWS documentation website for more details]
March 7, 2018	Updated the Frequently Viewed Amazon MQ Topics section.
March 6, 2018	Added the following note throughout this guide:Using the `mq.t2.micro` instance type is subject to * CPU credits and baseline performance*—with the ability to *burst* above the baseline level. If your application requires *fixed performance*, consider using an `mq.m4.large` instance type.
March 1, 2018	[See the AWS documentation website for more details]
February 28, 2018	Corrected image display in GitHub.
February 27, 2018	In addition to HTML, PDF, and Kindle, the Amazon MQ Developer Guide is available on GitHub. To leave feedback, choose the GitHub icon in the upper right-hand corner. ner.
February 26, 2018	[See the AWS documentation website for more details]

Date	Documentation Update
February 22, 2018	Clarified and corrected the information in the following sections: [See the AWS documentation website for more details]
February 21, 2018	Corrected the Java code in the following sections: [See the AWS documentation website for more details]
February 20, 2018	Clarified and corrected the information in the Amazon MQ Security and Best Practices for Amazon MQ sections.
February 19, 2018	[See the AWS documentation website for more details]
February 16, 2018	[See the AWS documentation website for more details]
February 15, 2018	[See the AWS documentation website for more details]
February 14, 2018	Updated the following sections:[See the AWS documentation website for more details]
February 13, 2018	[See the AWS documentation website for more details]
February 2, 2018	Created the Frequently Viewed Amazon MQ Topics section.
January 25, 2018	[See the AWS documentation website for more details]
January 24, 2018	[See the AWS documentation website for more details]
January 19, 2018	Updated the information in the Apache ActiveMQ Resources section.
January 18, 2018	Clarified and corrected the information in the Limits in Amazon MQ section.
January 17, 2018	Reinstated the recommendation to prefer virtual destinations over durable subscriptions, with an improved explanation.
January 11, 2018	[See the AWS documentation website for more details]
January 3, 2018	Added DescribeConfigurationRevision to the API Authentication and Authorization for Amazon MQ section.
December 15, 2017	Removed the recommendation against durable subscriptions from the Best Practices for Amazon MQ section.
December 8, 2017	[See the AWS documentation website for more details]
December 7, 2017	[See the AWS documentation website for more details]
December 5, 2017	[See the AWS documentation website for more details]
December 4, 2017	[See the AWS documentation website for more details]
December 1, 2017	[See the AWS documentation website for more details]

AWS Glossary

For the latest AWS terminology, see the AWS Glossary in the *AWS General Reference*.

www.ingramcontent.com/pod-product-compliance
Lightning Source LLC
LaVergne TN
LVHW082040050326
832904LV00005B/257